Design and Build Your Own
DOLL'S HOUSES

DESIGN AND BUILD YOUR OWN DOLL'S HOUSES

BERYL ARMSTRONG

THE APPLE PRESS

A QUINTET BOOK

Published by The Apple Press
6 Blundell Street
London N7 9BH

ISBN 1-85076-468-9

This book was designed and produced by
Quintet Publishing Limited
6 Blundell Street
London N7 9BH

Creative Director: Richard Dewing
Designer: Pete Laws
Project Editor: Helen Denholm
Editor: Lydia Darbyshire
Photographer: Nick Nicholson

Typeset in Great Britain by
Central Southern Typesetters, Eastbourne
Manufactured in Singapore by
Eray Scan Pte. Ltd.
Printed in Singapore by
Star Standard Pte. Ltd.

CONTENTS

INTRODUCTION

Everyone makes mistakes when they are trying a new skill, and the best results are always achieved when we learn from each other.

Too often, though, experts seem to forget the multitude of problems that confront newcomers to a hobby, and making doll's houses is no exception. As a result, I learned mainly by trial and error. My book, therefore, assumes that you are creating your first doll's house and explains many of the initial problems that other books do not mention; at the same time it offers some useful tips and ideas for more experienced makers. Because there are always several ways to approach each step, the alternatives and the pros and cons of each are explained. It is for you to choose the method that best suits your temperament, ability and aims. The house can then truly be said to be your very own.

The brief underlying this book was to make a house that would have universal appeal. I decided that the completed house would be weatherboarded, a finish that is widely used and can cover many architectural styles – a hideaway cabin, a chalet, a country cottage, a town house, a Tudor manor or a wealthy merchant's residence.

My original plans were changed and updated frequently during the building as I developed more practical methods of achieving different effects or found ways of giving the house more aesthetic appeal. Do not be afraid to experiment or use your instinct for creation. This is your house, and I can only guide you through the building stages.

Specialist miniaturist suppliers are not always within easy reach, so, with few exceptions, I have used basic materials throughout. Someone, somewhere is no doubt selling every conceivable, ready-made item for use in building a doll's house, but if cost and self-satisfaction are important, no aspect is too difficult to undertake yourself, even if you are a newcomer to the hobby.

I am not a professional. I have made the same mistakes that you are likely to make. Most of the tools I use are basic do-it-yourself tools that are found in most houses, but home-made gadgets are cheap and invaluable. Problem solving while creating each building is part of the fun.

Before you embark on making your first doll's house, you should heed the warning: "Doll's houses become addictive!"

You may decide to make a doll's house because you remember the one you had as a child; because you have fond memories of granny's old home; because you want to design the home of your dreams; or because you have an urge to create. Whatever your reason, working with miniatures will stretch your imagination and tax your ingenuity. Modelmaking is a craft, but one that everyone can enjoy.

OPPOSITE The completed doll's house that is built, stage by stage, in this book.

1
GETTING STARTED

The choice of style is almost infinite. You can make anything from a simple box room to a large mansion, and doll's houses can be built to represent every architectural period. Each country has its own architecture and history from which you can draw inspiration.

Most of the commercially made furnishings that used to be available were Victorian, but as the popularity of Tudor, Georgian and 1930s styles grew, manufacturers and suppliers have adapted to the new market. Someone, somewhere will be making whatever you need, either the items themselves in miniature perfection or the specialist materials needed to make them.

Study the craft magazines, explore the shops and attend as many of the doll's house exhibitions and fairs as you can. You will gradually find a path through the maze. If you have one nearby, join a club. The friendly, cooperative atmosphere in the doll's house world is wonderful, and clubs and workshops are becoming increasingly widespread, although some areas are less well served than others.

Study as many different architectural styles as you can until you find one that appeals to you. The real *aficionados* of the doll's house world choose a date and collect only the items that are authentic to that particular time. Most of us, however, are more likely to have a favourite style

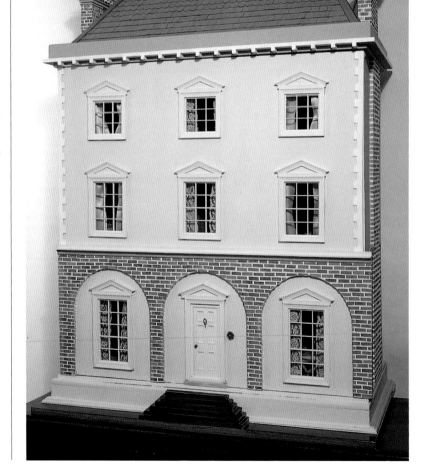

RIGHT The imposing Queen Anne mansion was made from a basic kit.

ABOVE This house started life long ago as a child's toy, and what was a derelict building has been transformed into a Tudor hall.

RIGHT The San Francisco house was built with a rear opening because its frontage is so elaborate.

OPPOSITE The original house has been extended, just as we add extensions to our modern homes.

of architecture, which we will furnish, as we do with our own houses, with whatever takes our fancy to give an overall pleasing effect.

Deciding on the size is important. The standard gauge for miniatures is 1:12 – i.e., 1 in (2.5 cm) to 1 ft (30 cm) – and when you come to furnish your doll's house and people it with dolls, you will find that commercially made items and kits are made to that scale. Do you want to make one

ABOVE The Bavarian chalet was created from a wooden wine box and was actually built in Bavaria.

LEFT The Victorian street scene was intended as one long building, but before assembly it was divided into a separate shop and a house for easy transport.

LEFT West Green Manor evolved from a plan for an eight-room house into a 15-room mansion during the building. No aspect of building a doll's house is too difficult, even for a newcomer to the hobby.

ABOVE All doll's houses are based on a simple box shape.

single room or a 20-room mansion? It is all very well allowing your original plans to evolve, as my first house, West Green Manor did, from eight rooms to 15, but you must think of the consequences. Do you have sufficient space to house such a large building? A doll's house as large as West Green Manor is likely to end up homeless if it is intended as a family heirloom.

If you live in a small house or flat, single box rooms or miniature shops and pubs are more practical, and they look most attractive when stored on shelves. Another consideration is that ambitiously large projects need more building space, whereas the construction of a single box can be undertaken on the kitchen table.

ABOVE AND RIGHT Shops and pubs have great creative potential.

ABOVE AND RIGHT Miniature scenes set in picture frames are perfect if your home is too small to accommodate a full-scale doll's house.

LEFT These models have been painted to accentuate the different styles of roofs. The shape you choose will govern the height of your tallest walls.

DO IT YOURSELF

No kit or ready-built house will fully meet your expectations, and by the time you have re-designed much of the detail you will be left with little more than a basic box. Even if you have no experience whatsoever, doing everything yourself still seems to be the best solution. Several firms sell plans, but if you study enough doll's houses you will see that you can start with a simple box shape and elaborate on the basic design as you gain experience.

If the task seems daunting, it is worth bearing in mind that most doll's house additions such as window frames, doors, shutters, bricks and tiles, are all commercially available. If you have a strong image of your house in mind, you will probably find that to make it exactly right you will want to build all the details yourself.

PLANNING AHEAD

Have you chosen the style and size of the house you wish to build? If you cannot find a printed picture of your ideal, draw a rough sketch of how you imagine it might look. Now draw this house to a conveniently reduced scale on a sheet of graph paper, remembering to draw it from all perspectives. The design will depend on whether you want gables and, if so, whether they are to be at either end, in the centre front or to one side. How many floors do you want to include? Do you want a flat roof, or one that is pitched or hipped, or would you prefer a mansard style? Will there be additional windows at the side or the back?

What size are the rooms to be and how many? Do not make them too small. Even the 12 × 12 in (30 × 30 cm) rooms in West Green Manor are not really large enough to give scope for exciting furnishings.

These five graphs show the dimensions of the house from all sides. You must draw a scale plan of your house on graph paper before you start building.

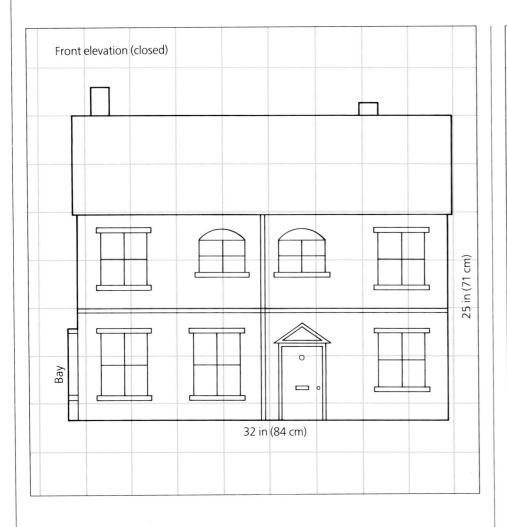

Front elevation (closed)

Bay

25 in (71 cm)

32 in (84 cm)

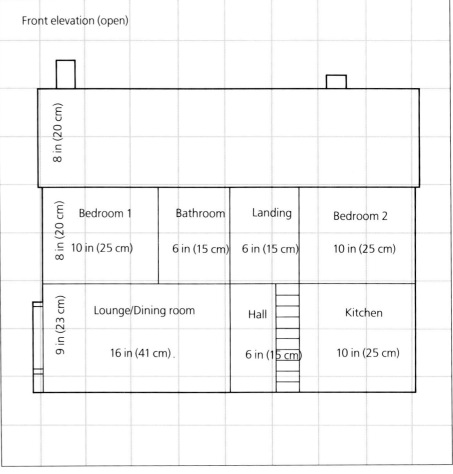

Front elevation (open)

8 in (20 cm)

Bedroom 1	Bathroom	Landing	Bedroom 2
10 in (25 cm)	6 in (15 cm)	6 in (15 cm)	10 in (25 cm)

8 in (20 cm)

Lounge/Dining room	Hall	Kitchen
16 in (41 cm)	6 in (15 cm)	10 in (25 cm)

9 in (23 cm)

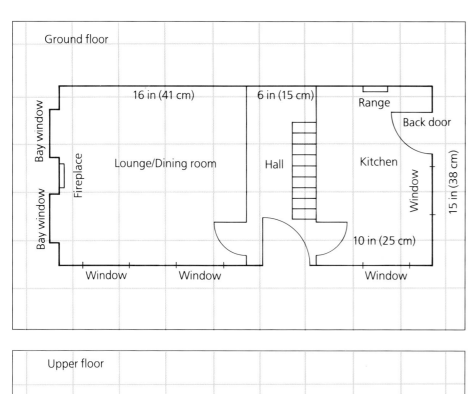

Ground floor

Bay window

Bay window

Bay window

Fireplace

16 in (41 cm)

6 in (15 cm)

Range

Back door

Lounge/Dining room

Hall

Kitchen

Window

15 in (38 cm)

10 in (25 cm)

Window

Window

Window

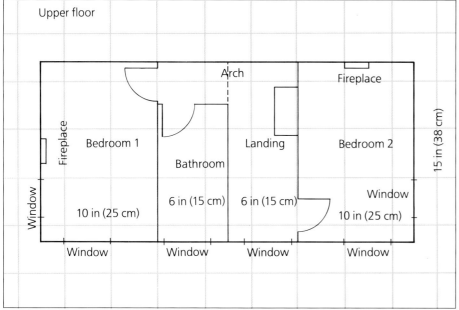

Upper floor

Fireplace

Window

Bedroom 1

10 in (25 cm)

Bathroom

6 in (15 cm)

Arch

Landing

6 in (15 cm)

Fireplace

Bedroom 2

Window

10 in (25 cm)

15 in (38 cm)

Window

Window

Window

Window

Left side wall

Right side wall

ABOVE Staggered stairs need an enlarged stairwell, which takes away half the usable floor space. However, twisted stairs are sometimes essential if the hall is tiny.

LEFT A small room offers less space for creative furnishings.

Another factor that you need to take into account when you are planning the overall dimensions is that a doll's house needs to be at least 15 in (38 cm) deep to accommodate a straight staircase with 3 in (7.5 cm) wide doors off the hall to the rooms. Entrance halls and upper landings can provide interesting areas to furnish without enlarging the overall size of the baseboard. If you want staggered stairs, you will lose half the floorspace so if this is your first doll's house, it is advisable to make a straight staircase – it won't be such a strain on your nervous system.

ABOVE You might consider placing the staircase in a large room if you need to reduce the overall width of your building. Be careful when planning the depth of rooms – if they are too deep they are difficult to reach into without knocking things.

The large rooms in the Sussex farmhouse are 13½ in (34.5 cm) wide and 18 in (46 cm) deep. If they are too deep, you will have problems reaching the back, so 14 × 15 in (35.5 × 36 cm) is a good compromise. This size gives you scope to divide a room – to create a small bathroom or night nursery, for example. The hallways need to be at least 7½ in (19 cm) wide if you have more than two floors, which requires double staircases, but 5½ in (14 cm) is sufficient for two-storey houses.

If space is really at a premium, you can sacrifice the landing room by having a half-flight, with the next flight doubling back. This will need a hallway that is only 5 in (12.5 cm) wide. In such circumstances you might decide not to have a hall or landing at all, but instead, to site the staircase in a living room so that you can keep a single flight of stairs.

The height of the rooms will range between 8 in (20 cm) and 10 in (25 cm). Remember that the main rooms will be larger and have higher ceilings than basements or attics.

Another question you must consider at the outset is how and where you want to guide your lighting wires. The wiring is probably something you do not even want to think about when you haven't started to build a house, but it is an aspect that you should consider at the outset. It is both easy and safe to install the lighting when you know the basics.

However anxious you are to make a start, do not skimp on the planning stages, because they will save you hours of unnecessary alterations and wasted wood. When I first started to make doll's houses I did not think far enough ahead, and it cost money and effort to solve problems that would not have arisen had I thought out all the stages before I began.

When you have designed your house, draw the three sides, and the ground and upper floors to full size on sheets of brown paper and cut them out. These paper patterns are only a guide so they do not have to be accurate, but they will indicate the amount of wood you will need. Forget the front at this stage because the shell is the most important part.

2
MATERIALS

WOOD

Your next questions will probably be the same as mine were initially: what kind of wood? How thick should it be? How much will I need?

Thin plywood can vary considerably in quality, and to prevent splintering it is worth paying extra. Plywood is light in weight and easy to cut with a fine-toothed, sharp saw. Always cut with the side that it going to show uppermost so that any splintering along the edges can usually be hidden. A good sanding smooths down the rough edges.

When thin plywood is held with the grain running vertically it bends sideways. This is a useful characteristic if you need curved surfaces.

Wrap thin, flexible ply around a former, then stick other layers on top until you have a wall of the required strength.

Wood that is only about ⅛ in (2–4 mm) thick is liable to warp on the grain. You should avoid thin ply for fixtures to which items such as screw rings for curtain rods or door hinges are to be fixed. It is just not deep enough for a screw or panel pin to bite on.

Medium density fibreboard (MDF) comes in standard thicknesses up to about ¾ in (18 mm); 1⁄16 in (2 mm) is too thin, but you will find that ¼ in (6 mm) is useful. Unlike hardboard, MDF has two shiny surfaces and is dense all through. It is comparatively cheap and extremely easy to cut

RIGHT Medium density fibreboard (MDF) has its supporters and its uses.

FAR RIGHT Plywood is available in many thicknesses and qualities.

and shape. Its disadvantages are that it generates a lot of dust when it is cut and sanded. Because it is softer board, you can only screw into it once – there is no bite for a second try. Also, the surface is apt to peel off if you have stuck a feature to it that comes under a lot of pressure – a small shelf that is often knocked, for example, or hinges on opening doors.

MDF is ideal for small buildings, baseboards or roofs if you cover it with bricks or tiles. It is a matter of taste whether you use it throughout for a large house, but if cost is of the essence or ease of cutting is important, then take the practical view and use it. The weight is similar to that of wood.

ABOVE Round houses are built by adding layers of thin, flexible plywood until the walls are strong.

LEFT Most doll's houses are built from woods like plywood and medium density fibreboard (MDF), which are widely available.

RIGHT Screws have many advantages over panel pins when it comes to holding a house in shape.

Birch ply is a quality wood, which is available in various standard thicknesses. It is smooth, makes good, strong doll's houses, rarely splinters and holds glue and screws firmly. Its only disadvantages are the price and the extra energy that is required for cutting. A good workable thickness is ¼ in (6 mm).

How much wood do you need? How big is your house? Ask your supplier what size sheets he stocks and which way the grain will lie. With string, mark out the sheet size on your house floor and lay the brown paper pattern inside this area to judge the quantity of wood you will need.

SCREWS

When I first started to make doll's houses, I was reluctant to glue any part permanently until I was 100 per cent certain that I wouldn't need to dismantle the house to add a feature that I had not foreseen. Even so, I had to resort to the mallet on several occasions to part a well-glued section.

While you are feeling your way in your first house you will no doubt screw and unscrew, trim, recut and rasp until you have a reasonable

framework. This is tough on your hands and even more expensive in terms of screws.

The secret is to take two drill bits – one that is the thickness of the screw shank and the other, the pilot, a size smaller. Drill a full-depth hole with the thinner bit and a shallow hole, the length of the screw shank, with the other one. This will allow you to ease the screw in without tearing the wood and with less strain on your hands. It also enables you to remove and rescrew several times. If the hole becomes too big, a sliver of wood or matchstick will give an extra bite.

The recognized method of screwing into the end grain of wood, especially ply, is to insert a plug made of dowel on the flat side so that the screw is held in the strong side grain of the dowel. This is a useful tip to prevent hinges from tearing the plywood layers apart.

Brass screws are more expensive than steel ones and they are softer. Brass screws are not really suitable for door hinges because the heads can crumble under the constant strain, leaving you with an unsupported hinge.

Screws are expensive and you are bound to use more than you anticipate, so keep a good stock in various sizes. Thin screws are not so easy to find as those for normal household use.

Most experts suggest that you use panel pins. You may have problems though, as they are apt to bend over with the hammering or become so badly slanted that they come out of the side. When you are just starting, mistakes are bound to happen and it is more encouraging to know that the construction can be taken apart before the final gluing. Distorted walls caused by uneven cutting or warping can be forced into line and held in place with screws if they are not too far out of true.

Even after making many houses, I still find that screws are more practical than pins. It is easier to turn a screwdriver in confined spaces and in awkward corners than to raise a hammer.

GENERAL TOOLS

This list of tools may look formidable, but these items are really basic DIY tools similar to those used in the photographs. Even if you do not already have them around your home, they can be easily obtained from general hobby shops.

Expensive power tools, while useful, are definitely not essential. If you want to treat yourself, the vibratory fretsaw is probably the most versatile. Even the cheapest model is finger safe and has a long service life.

The 12-in (30-cm) frame, hand-held fretsaw is too unwieldy without a special table and, like the vibratory fretsaw, is too restrictive when it comes to cutting out windows. A frame around 6 in (15 cm) in size will involve fewer blade replacements and ensure a cooler temper! Even a small coping saw is adequate for many finer jobs.

Saws You will need the following saws to make the basic doll's house described here. A large saw for cutting sheets of wood; a small hobby saw for cutting trim – these usually come with replaceable blades; a small fretsaw or coping saw for carving shapes; and a keyhole or power jigsaw for cutting out areas too far inside the sheet for a fretsaw – for example, windows.

Knives A general-purpose craft knife can be used for many cutting and trimming tasks, while a hobby craft knife, which has a smaller blade, is useful for work in confined spaces. Both these knives have replaceable blades.

Drills A hand-turned or hobby power drill with all sizes of bits is needed for screw holes, especially for countersinking, and an Archimedes' drill for small pilot holes – for internal door hinges, for example – is invaluable.

LEFT A plug of dowel set into ply will hold screw hinges firmly and prevent them from tearing the plywood layers.

Files These are available in all shapes and sizes – flat, half-round, round, square, triangular and so on. Use whatever is available, but a large flat file and a set of small hobby files are the most useful.

Screwdrivers You will need a general selection of these in a range of sizes.

Extras You will also find that you will need the following at various stages: a bench vice, small clamps, tweezers, a mitre block, sandpaper, fine-grade steel wool, pencils, an accurate ruler and a wide steel ruler for a cutting edge.

GLUES

The number of glues on the market has become bewildering, but if you buy three basic types you will cover most jobs: PVA white wood adhesive, which is water based; an all-purpose clear adhesive, which is spirit based; and a quick-drying contact adhesive – either general purpose or non-drip.

3
MAKING A BOX

Before you build a doll's house you should appreciate the principle of constructing a basic box. You may want to make a simple box room or a shop before you embark on a large building, which is, in effect, a series of boxes stacked together to form a house. The outside of a house is one large box divided into sections, called rooms.

The sides of your box should overlap the back, which should fit snugly between the two side walls but should be the same height. The base should fit between the walls and the back panel. This involves quite a tedious calculation, which needs time to master. Forget about the front-opening door for now.

Use ¼ in (6 mm) wood and no. 2 screws. The sides and back of the box need to be the same height; the side walls are ¼ in (6 mm) deeper than the baseboard, which is ½ in (12 mm) narrower than the roof and ¼ in (6 mm) less deep. The back panel is exactly the same width as the baseboard and the same height as the sides. The roof sits on top of the side walls and the back.

Because all ply is liable to warp, it is advisable to let the grain of the wood run vertically on upright sections and along the length of the longer, horizontal pieces. The direction of the grain is not as important with small, square sections.

Confused? Take heart, it isn't as complicated as it sounds. If you do not want a box room just yet, try making a small box to learn the basic principles, and keep it as a sample for future use.

You will probably find the diagram and illustrations clearer to follow than the written instructions.

ABOVE All doll's houses are basically boxes divided into rooms. This example was built from an old wine box.

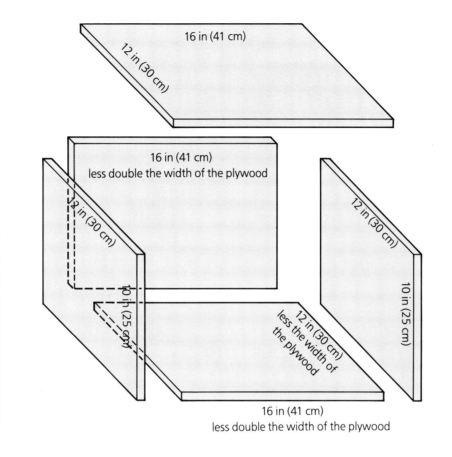

16 in (41 cm)

12 in (30 cm)

16 in (41 cm)
less double the width of the plywood

12 in (30 cm)

12 in (30 cm)

12 in (30 cm)

10 in (25 cm)

10 in (25 cm)

12 in (30 cm)
less the width of
the plywood

16 in (41 cm)
less double the width of the plywood

16 in (41 cm)
less double the width of the plywood

LEFT The external measurements of the finished box are 16 × 12 × 10 in (41 × 30 × 25 cm). The base sits between the sides and the back, while the back sits between the sides but not actually on the base. The roof rests on the sides and along the top edge of the back. All edges are flush at the front, so that a door may be added later if wished.

Assembly

When you have cut out the five pieces of wood, hold them together one at a time to check that you have measured them correctly.

Now lay one side flat on your working surface, butted against the baseboard. The side is ¼ in (6 mm) deeper, so push them both against another straight edge to make sure that the front edges are flush.

Use a ruler to draw short lines at intervals across the two pieces where you will need screws. Three or four screws on each side is quite adequate. Follow the pencil lines round to the edge of the baseboard. Double-check that the extended lines still marry up, and mark the centre point along the lines you have drawn. These pencil marks give you the position for drilling holes. Hold the base in a vice, and drill a hole with the thinner of the two drill bits (see page 26). Be careful that you keep the drill upright; if you do not, the hole will pierce the flat surface.

Draw a line ¼ in (6 mm) inside the edge of the side wall. Mark a ⅛ in (3 mm) centre point along each of the lines you drew to indicate the positions of the screws. Drill a hole right through with the thicker drill bit, then use the countersink bit to gouge the wood on the outer face so that the screw head will lie just slightly below the surface.

ASSEMBLING A BOX

1 This box room is 16 in (41 cm) wide, 10 in (25 cm) high and 12 in (30 cm) deep. Before you assemble it, check that you have cut the component parts to the correct size.

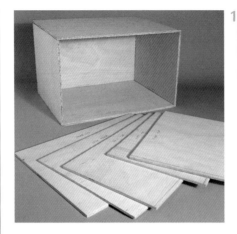

2 Make sure that the front edges are level, then draw lines at intervals across both sections to indicate where the screws will marry up.

3 Start by assembling one wall and the base.

4 The rear wall is added next, followed by the second wall.

5 Finally, the roof is screwed into the top of the walls to complete the box.

Repeat this with all the sections that are to be joined together. When all the drill holes have been prepared, begin to assemble the pieces, starting with the baseboard and one side. Screw the rear panel into place, then the other side.

If all fits well you can move to the roof. If it does not, you should dismantle and start again by drilling fresh holes that marry up. When everything is correctly aligned, unscrew, run wood glue along the edges and rescrew. The basic box is ready for the roof.

Try the roof out for size and shave off any overlapping wood until it fits accurately. As before, allow for the ¼ in (6 mm) thickness, find a centre point and drill the wider hole and the countersink. Lay the panel on top of the walls. You can tape it in place to stop it from slipping. Drill

with the thinner bit into the upper edge of the side walls, using the roof holes as a guide. Again, when everything is correctly positioned, unscrew, glue, then rescrew.

Now you have made a box, you can go ahead and make a doll's house as complicated as you wish!

A front made as one removable section is usually best for box rooms. If you have a hinged door you can, if necessary, strengthen the front upright edges of the frame by gluing then screwing an extra piece of beading to take the thicker hinge screws.

It is best to use ¼ in (6 mm) birch ply for basic house building and approximately ⅛ in (4 mm) for roof sections and any smaller internal partitions that do not require hinges or screws. Some miniaturists use ⅓ in (9 mm) throughout, but these houses are extremely heavy and are not practical for most of us.

ABOVE AND RIGHT Identical boxes can be used in an almost infinite number of ways as these shops demonstrate. They were part of a 27-room shopping emporium.

MAKING THE FRAMEWORK

When you have successfully made a basic box, go back to your plan of the house and the paper patterns that you cut out. Lay these on the sheet of plywood and shuffle them around until you find the most economical arrangement. Remember, however, that laying one piece against the grain could be an expensive mistake if your wood warps either during assembly or if the doll's house sits in a damp room.

When you are satisfied, draw the sections accurately and directly onto the wood using a pencil, steel ruler and set square. Label each piece before you cut it out. The room dividers need to be fractionally taller than the space between the floors because you may later decide to gouge grooves for them to slot in place. Cut out all the sections. Do not be disheartened by your first effort: everyone complains that they cannot cut a straight line, even after they have made many houses. Most people do not possess or have the space to house a large saw bench with a guide, but the use of screws will enable you to rectify some mistakes. A long length of factory-cut beading or something similar can be used as a straight edge, and you can whittle down the bumps with a craft knife. Give everything a good finish with sandpaper.

By now you will be surrounded by a jigsaw puzzle of house building sections, each labelled in pencil. It is especially important to indicate which pieces are to be used to the left or right, at the front or back, and at the top or bottom. Be careful to draw in the exact positions of the floors in the same way you marked the position of screw holes in the box – lay the wood flat and draw a line over the two sections. All the drill holes must marry up along these lines.

ABOVE The basic framework. The floors fit between the end walls with the room partitions just slotted in place. They will be permanently fixed later.

CUTTING OUT THE HOUSE SHAPES

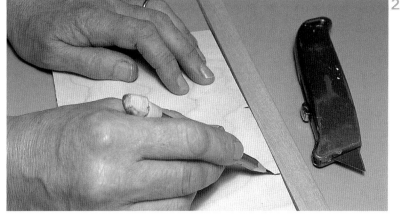

1 Draw the full-size measurements for all the sections of your house accurately onto the wood.

2 A piece of factory-cut beading makes a practical straight edge against which to check that your sides are straight. Mark the sections of uneven cutting that need whittling down with a craft knife.

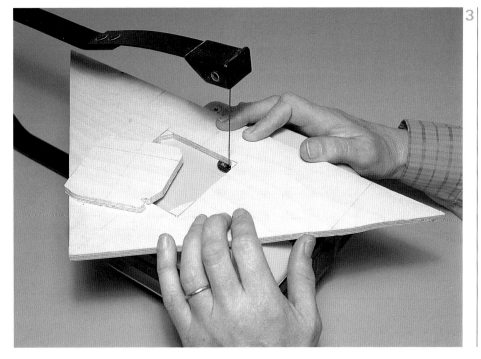

3 In the sections that need holes for doors or windows, drill a hole in the area to be removed and thread the fretsaw blade through it. Cut away the waste by following straight lines and curving round the corners. Then cut neatly into each corner.

ASSEMBLING THE SHELL OF THE HOUSE

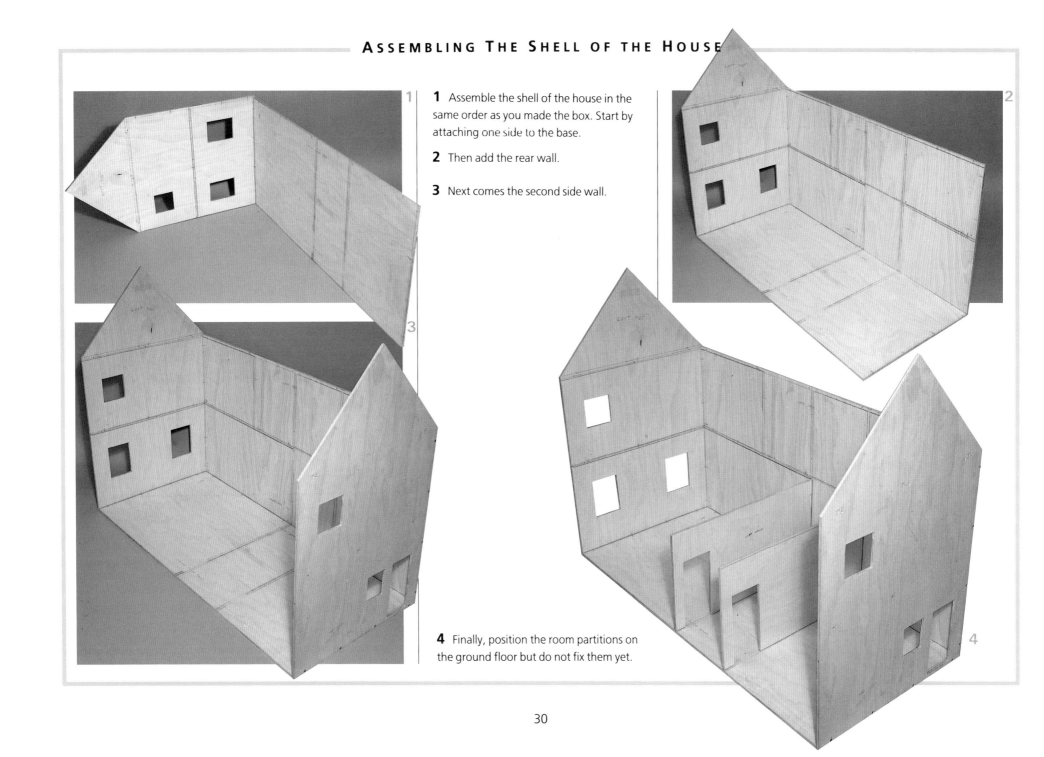

1 Assemble the shell of the house in the same order as you made the box. Start by attaching one side to the base.

2 Then add the rear wall.

3 Next comes the second side wall.

4 Finally, position the room partitions on the ground floor but do not fix them yet.

Up to now you have solid pieces of wood with no openings for doors, windows or fireplaces. Now that your walls are cut to size, you will find it easier to gauge exactly where you want these features and how many you want. The first house I made had 26 windows, nine internal doors and six open fireplaces. Making this number is not a problem but it is time-consuming.

If you are cutting openings in a sheet of wood and, say, the windows are too far in for the fretsaw, you will find an electric jigsaw useful, or for the faint-hearted, a simple keyhole saw. A vibratory fretsaw has many uses. You can thread the blade through inside spaces and it frees both hands for guiding the wood. The drawback is that is has a 14 in (37 cm) limit, so a single blade is needed for larger areas. Make the windows any size you wish, but around 3 × 4 in (7.5 × 10 cm) is average. When you are planning, do not forget to calculate the space needed for the window surrounds and curtains, especially if two windows are separated by an internal chimney breast.

Doorways must be a realistic 5½–6 in (14–15 cm) high, and you should allow a width of 3 in (7.5 cm), including the opening and its archi-traves.

Drill a hole in the area to be removed to give access for the fretsaw blade. Chisel three holes together to make a slot for the wider blades. Roughly cut away the waste by following the straight pencil lines but swerving round the corners until the centre block comes away. Now you can cut neatly into each corner, starting on a straight line and working from each direction.

If the window and door holes are not true to shape, use a set square, craft knife and sandpaper to give sharp right-angled corners. Do not worry if the holes vary in size by a fraction because the windows will be set individually. However, if you are buying ready-made door and window fittings, your holes will have to fit the manufacturer's specifications.

At this stage, too, you will have to decide if you are going to have internal chimney breasts for each fire or external flues up the outside walls, which involves cutting the fire holes before assembly.

The next job is to assemble the shell of the house in exactly the same way as you made the box, although it will be much bigger. It is less cumbersome if you work with the house lying on its back. You will have to insert all the floors in the same manner as you fitted the ground floor, because the top floor will be sitting between the gables, and the sloping roof will, in effect, be the box lid. Draw lines on each floor to indicate where you wish to divide these areas into rooms. At this stage you can screw in the upper ceiling, but do not glue anything. You should now have what looks rather like an open bookcase.

I hope you have done better than my first effort. I screwed and unscrewed, drilled and redrilled countless times. My shaky line cutting also meant that I had a lot of planing and rasping to do as well. In some pieces I had so many false holes, I had to circle the right holes with pencil so that I could be sure of putting the screws into their final resting places.

The main point at this stage is to make sure that the large back sheet fits accurately between the sides and against the floors. Do not worry about minor gaps. They can be plugged with a mix of fine sawdust and wood glue, which can be used like plastic wood. Never waste anything, not even your sawdust!

Spend some time studying the framework of your house because now is your last chance to change your mind and improve on your original design. Do you want to add an extension, such as a conservatory leading off the rear of the lounge? Or perhaps you would like a large bay window or a turret room. I chose to include an outside kitchen door and window because I may decide to add an extension here at some later date. Although this project is designed to demonstrate how to make a standard shape house, you can elaborate on it as you wish.

THE INTERNAL FLOORS AND WALLS

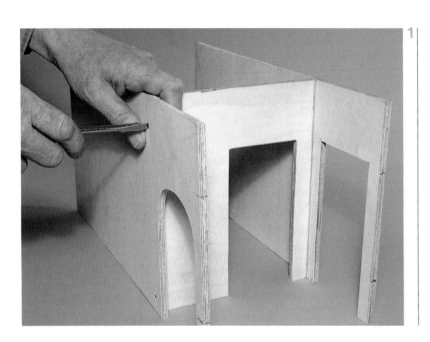

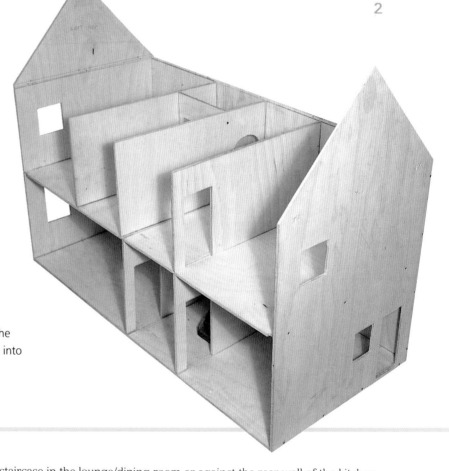

1 Once you have inserted the upper ceiling (screwed but not glued) and before you put in the room partitions, make the bathroom as a single unit, leaving a realistic corridor behind the room.

2 From this angle you can see how the bathroom fits in, with a door opening into the hall.

This is the point at which I redrew my original graph plans. The room dividers had to be moved to balance the rooms on the two floors. I also opted for windows on the sides of the bedrooms. All of these would have been extremely difficult to include if I had glued the framework first and demonstrates the benefit of using screws.

If a width of 3 ft (over 90 cm) is too large for your display table, you can scale the house down. You could eliminate the hallway and put the staircase in the lounge/dining room or against the rear wall of the kitchen.

Alternatively, you can reduce the width of the main room, although I would advise you to keep to the 15 in (38 cm) depth. Other options are to make the house taller by adding a third floor or to create rooms in the loft space. If you have already cut the wood to the measurements given here, all you need do now is to cut the same size strip from each of the floors and the back wall.

5
THE STAIRCASE

Now that you are satisfied with the basic framework, the next challenge is to make a staircase. Until this is made, you cannot cut out the exact position of the stairwell hole on the upper landings.

Making the stairs is comparatively easy. The hard part is adding the banisters and top rail and adjusting the height as they near the ceiling. This stage, however, can be left until you have decorated your house.

With the narrow hallway in this project, make a straight staircase fixed to one wall as this gives stability and more space for furniture.

For this size of house I would suggest you make the staircase around 2¼ in (5.5 cm) wide. You will need approximately 14 stairs cut from a strip of ¾ in (2 cm) triangle-shaped wood. Stick the wide bases close together on a length of ¹⁄₁₆ in (2 mm) ply, 14 in (35.5 cm) long and 2¼ in (5.5 cm) wide. Do not forget to stain the stairs before gluing if you do not intend using paint. Stain is not absorbed by glue, and you will be left with

RIGHT The simplest stairs are made by gluing strips of triangle beading to ¹⁄₁₆ in (2 mm) ply.

blotchy patches if you try to apply after gluing. Cover the rough sides of your stairs with strips of ply.

Another popular method is to stick solid blocks of wood on top of each other, each block set slightly back from the step beneath it.

A more sophisticated method for making a staircase is to use stringers, treads and risers as in real life. Cut out two stringers in ⅛ in (3 mm) thick wood using the full-size pattern. The stair treads should measure ⅞ in (22 mm) deep by 2¼ in (5.5 cm) wide, while the risers should be slightly smaller – ⅝ × 2⅛ in (16 mm × 5 cm). Cut them in ¹⁄₁₆ in (2 mm) wood. Mahogany is more attractive than ply.

You will find it easier if you make a jig from wood to support the two stringers and to keep them parallel. The outside faces of the stringers should be fractionally less than 2¼ in (5.5 cm) apart. Stick the risers on first so they sit neatly on the stringers. Butt the treads up against the risers so that they protrude just a little over the front and one side of the stringer. You can buy strips of stair nosing to finish off the front edges neatly.

If you have opted for the simple method of using triangle beading or solid blocks, your next step will be less complicated if you make yourself a mock hallway from, say, a stiff cardboard box. All you need are two

ABOVE Solid blocks are often used in a small hall with minimal depth because they can be adjusted to any height. Unfortunately, they may not look realistic. More sophisticated stairs are made with stringers, risers and treads.

RIGHT You can use this diagram of a full-size stringer as a pattern to cut out the two stringers for your staircase, if you choose this method.

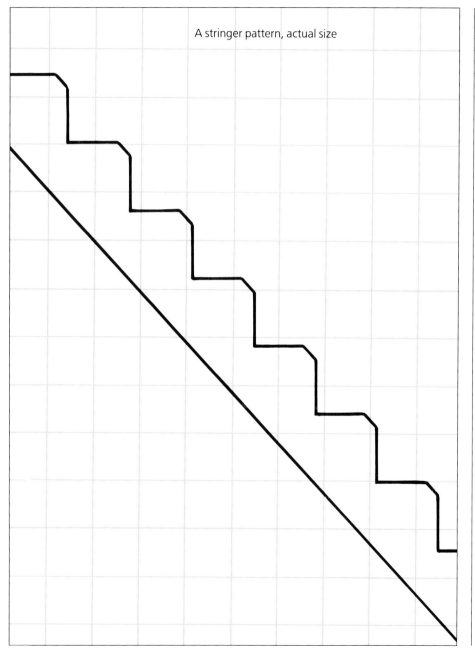

A stringer pattern, actual size

RIGHT A mock hallway made from a cardboard box is invaluable during the construction of a staircase. It is particularly useful when you come to add the banisters and handrail.

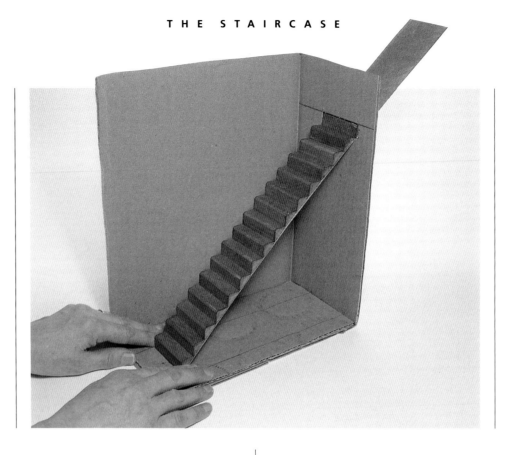

walls and a floor. Mark a line on the rear narrow wall that corresponds to your ceiling height. Cut a slit on and below the line so that you can slide the ⅟₁₆ in (2 mm) staircase ply and the top stair tread through it.

Move your stairs back and forth until the treads are horizontal, which will give an angle of around 45 degrees. The top tread will be stuck to the underside of your ceiling so, allowing for this, add an extra tread if necessary or take off one if you have too many. When you are satisfied that the staircase is level, make a line below the bottom tread.

Using your hall room divider as a guide, mark a line on the house floor to indicate where the stairs begin, beyond the inner doorway. Hold the top tread against the ceiling and pencil a line in front of this tread. The stairwell hole needs to be the width of your stairs and approximately 5½ in (14 cm) in front of your pencil line.

Do not place your stairway too far to the rear because you need an area where people can step off the stairs and turn to walk along the upper landing. The room doorway and staircase will take up around 12 in (30 cm) of your room, which is why you need a hallway that is at least 15 in (38 cm) deep. If you want to make a smaller house, you can, of course, save space by siting a door under the stairs.

Stairs to a third floor or to the roof space have to be set against the opposite landing wall and to rise in the reverse direction, so that, from the front, you will see the base rising to the ceiling. If you have more than two floors, your hallway needs to be 7½ in (19 cm) wide to take the double staircases.

Now dismantle your framework and cut out any areas where extensions are to be added and the hole for the stairwell.

LEFT If your house has more than two floors the hall must be wide enough to accommodate a double staircase and provide walking room for the occupants.

6
ADDING THE ROOM DIVIDERS

It is a good idea to gouge grooves for the upright room dividers. This is comparatively simple in theory if you are using birch ply.

Using a steel ruler and a sharp craft knife, make deep cuts into the floors, ceilings and back board along your pencilled lines. These should be ¼ in (6 mm) apart. Run a chisel between each pair of lines and the wood should come away to leave a smooth groove. The upright partition room walls can be trimmed to slide into the grooves, but should not be fixed at this stage. Merely slot them in and hold in place with tape if necessary. Grooving can be a somewhat hit and miss affair, so try it on a piece of scrap wood first. It is always easier to cut with the grain than across it. I managed to cut three grooves on this project before I gave up. Perhaps my chisel was not sharp enough or the wood was extra tough.

Only when you are satisfied with everything should you glue and screw the outer framework together. If your plans include unusual room features you could find it less difficult to work from above. If you decide to do this, do not glue the floors, but fully fit and decorate each level as if you are making a series of box rooms. You may prefer to paint or paper the ceiling and to drill lighting wire holes while it is on the work bench.

Always think one step ahead and sort out possible problems while you are doing a particular job. For example, if the hallway is deep and narrow, it is going to be difficult to decorate. Can you do it from above or by papering the partitions before you glue them into place? Do not forget to hang the internal doors and add doorknobs before decorating. Door and window architraves are added after papering.

LEFT If you would prefer your room dividers to run in channels, practise on scrap wood to see if your particular ply lends itself to having grooves cut in it.

I know from experience that trying to screw rings above the windows for curtain rods, especially for the window behind a chimney breast, is difficult. You would be wise to glaze and dress this window before the ceiling is fixed. Glue each ceiling only when that floor is complete. (See the guide order later in the book.)

Before gluing the horizontal dividers, remember to cut the front corners to take a strip down each side to give added support to the long hinges when they are eventually fitted. Alternatively, you may decide to use dowel plugs instead or to rely on the extra support outside the house.

If you do not want to make slotting grooves, skirting boards and ceiling coving will add support to a glued wall after the house is decorated. There is no need to groove the upper central section in this house because the rear bathroom wall acts as a stabilizer. Another possibility is to screw the partitions to the lower and upper floors and/or to the rear wall.

Your house should be taking shape now, but it will look rather odd with all those holes for windows, doors and fireplaces. Nevertheless, remember what your vision of a dream house looks like and keep working towards it.

By this stage you will have discovered that making a doll's house is fraught with "chicken and egg" situations. You cannot do this before you do that, yet you cannot do that before you have done this. As with a real house, there are seemingly endless decisions to be made about the order in which each stage should be tackled. At least we do not need realistic plumbing.

HANGING THE DOORS

Before you glue the room partitions permanently into position, make and hang the doors while you can work at your bench.

The doors will vary according to the style and period of your chosen house. In the first houses I made I experimented with different types of wood and card – you will find that discarded doors make good bed bases!

Lay the room partition with the door opening on a piece of card and draw around it. This will give you a template, which will be necessary if your opening is not 100 per cent accurate. Use this card pattern to cut a piece of good quality ⅛ in (4 mm) grained wood. Try it for size, sanding it down where necessary until it fits the doorway, with a slight clearance at the sides and top and a little more at the bottom to allow for the floor covering you will fit later.

If you want a country-style door, you could gouge vertical grooves in ply to simulate planks. I have tried this method, but I found that unless I merely scratched the surface, the wood tended to roughen on the uneven grain. Using good quality wood, though, gave an acceptable result. The neatest way is to add strips of narrow beading with a tiny gap between each length. These must, of course, be stained first, unless you intend to paint the door. Repeat on the other side so that the ⅛ in (4 mm) ply is a sandwich. Sand all the edges smooth. When your door is complete, check that it fits your doorway space, then it is ready for hanging.

If you want to go up-market and have a panelled door, start with the basic ply as before and stain it if required. Now glue the strips in any

MAKING DOORS IN DIFFERENT STYLES

1 Make card templates of your doors while the room partitions are on the workbench. Use these to cut out the pieces of ⅛ in (4 mm) ply to which you will add beading and/or panelling to both sides, in whatever style you choose.

2 For a country-style door you can groove planks in the door; some woods give better results than others.

3 A panelled door looks effective and can be made in any style you choose.

4 There have been many door styles over the centuries, and you have a wide choice of designs.

pattern, according to the style you want to have. Start with the vertical edges and fit the cross bars in between. If you want a larger panel then cut a square of ⅟₃₂in (1mm) ply that fits in the space with a small gap all round to give the impression of stepped edge beading.

These are the simplest doors for a beginner to make, but as you gain experience you will be able to make something more elaborate. You can either paint your door or stain it.

FITTING HIDDEN DOOR HINGES

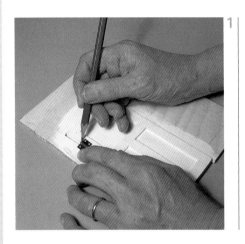

1 Mark the position of your hinge on the door with a pencil.

2 Hold the door firmly in a vice and gouge a seating for the hinge with a craft knife or chisel. Check the hinge fits, place the door in its frame again, mark the corresponding place for the hinge on the frame and gouge that out too.

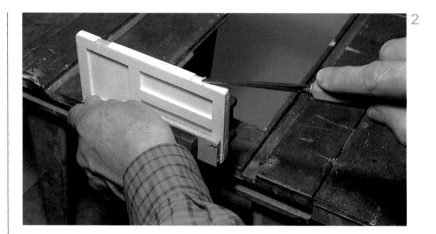

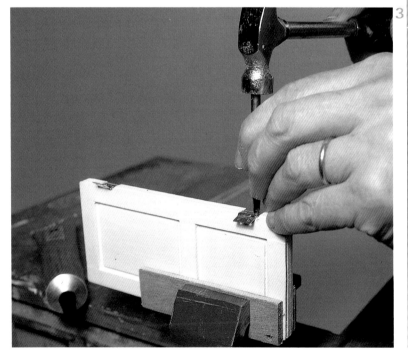

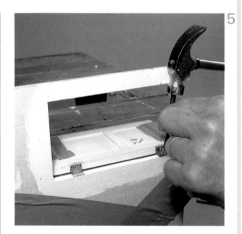

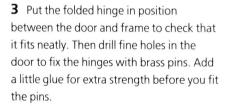

3 Put the folded hinge in position between the door and frame to check that it fits neatly. Then drill fine holes in the door to fix the hinges with brass pins. Add a little glue for extra strength before you fit the pins.

4 Pre-drill holes on the frame before tapping in the pins. An Archimedes' drill has many uses in building a doll's house.

5 Support the door at right angles to the frame before you tap the final pins into the frame.

1 Door and window architraves are cut at an angle of 45 degrees, but they are not glued in place until after decorating.

2 Newspaper column lines are useful guides for checking that mitred joints fit perfectly.

HINGES

Adding hidden hinges to a door is one of those jobs that, even when you know the theory back to front and do everything according to the rules, usually comes out far from perfect.

Lay your door in the gap you have cut from the room divider. Open the hinges and lay them flat over the two pieces. Draw pencil lines above and below the hinges on the door only. Using a craft knife or chisel, carefully gouge out an area on the thin inner edge that is just deep enough to seat the hinge in the gap. When it fits, mark up the corresponding area on the door frame and gouge that in the same way.

You should be able to fold the hinge and fit it in the two gouged sections. If all looks well, put the door in a vice and drill fine holes; you will find an Archimedes' drill useful here. A dab of glue will give further

ABOVE Simple hinges can be used if you cut the door slightly larger all around than the frame. Lay the hinges flat on the door, pinning the other halves to a strip of wood that is the same thickness. Glue and pin the strip to the wall, and your door is in place.

security for the hinges before you punch in brass pins. An impact adhesive is better than super glue because you can remove the hinge before it hardens if it is not quite right.

Fix both door hinges, top and bottom, before you attempt to glue and pin the other halves to the doorway. The door should swing freely and at least close. If it does not, you have probably not gouged out enough wood from the door or from the frame to allow for the protrusion of pin heads. If the groove is too deep, you will have to remove the hinges before the glue sets hard and pack out the recess.

If you feel you cannot cope with hidden hinges just yet, lay them flat across the front of the door and frame in the manner of a gate.

Another common method for hanging doors is to use dressmaker's steel pins. Drill a very fine hole in the top of the door as close to the corner as possible. Make a corresponding hole in the door frame. Press the pin hard into the door, cut off the head and poke the protruding pin up into the hole in the frame. Insert another pin into the bottom of the door and cut off the head. To hold it you will need to make a doorstep that will sit between the open frame. This means that the door needs to be slightly shorter than the frame.

If the door does not swing freely on its pin pivots, sand one long side edge to make it slightly rounded.

The architraves around the door frame are best added after you have wallpapered. The printed black rules in a newspaper or magazine are ideal for checking that your mitred corners are perfectly square.

Don't forget to add the doorknobs at this stage; it will be virtually impossible once the wall partitions are in place.

HANGING DOORS USING DRESSMAKER'S PINS

1 Cut out a door that is slightly shorter than the frame. Drill a fine hole as near to the corner of the door as you can.

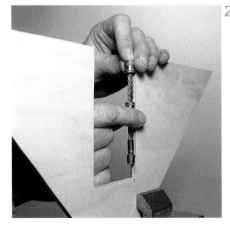

2 Drill a corresponding hole in the upper door frame.

3 Press dressmaker's steel pins into the top and bottom of the door and cut off the heads. Fit top pin into the upper hole in the frame.

4 The lower pin needs a step between the door jambs and the foot. Slightly round one long edge of the door so that it swings freely on its pivots.

8
WALLPAPERING

The whole question of decorating a doll's house raises additional questions about the sequence of individual steps. You will find it easier to decorate before the big front doors are added and will also probably encounter fewer problems if you decorate one floor at a time before you put the ceilings in place.

Are you considering introducing any permanent internal cupboards or fittings that would be less of a problem if you work from above? You may prefer to paint or paper the ceilings while they are flat on your workbench.

Always try to think one step ahead and anticipate possible problems. For example, the hallway and landing are deep and narrow, and they are going to be difficult to decorate. Can you do it from above or by papering the room partitions before you glue them in place? Remember, too, to hang and add doorknobs to your internal doors before you decorate.

Cut your paper to size before you actually stick it to the walls. Unless you have spare wallpaper, make templates first from scrap paper.

Start with the ceiling. Either paint it with a silk emulsion or use an embossed wallpaper to simulate plaster rendering. Never use gloss paint or heavy varnish on a doll's house, inside or outside, because it seems to break the illusion of a true-to-size miniature.

Cut the paper for the back wall slightly wider than the actual wall so that when you paste it in place it comes round the corner by about ½ in (12 mm). Put paste on the wooden walls, then on the paper.

The paper for the side walls should be cut to the exact size so that it fits right into the corner, overlapping the flap of back paper. This will

PAPERING CEILINGS, AND BACK AND SIDE WALLS

1 Paper and/or paint the ceiling first. Drill holes for the ceiling lights and glue on the roses. These can be made effectively from modelling clay or bought. Cut away the waste paper over the stairwell when the adhesive is dry.

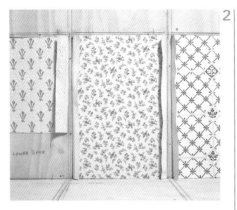

2 Paper the back walls first, leaving the edges longer and unglued so that they can come around the corner onto the partition walls to hide the join.

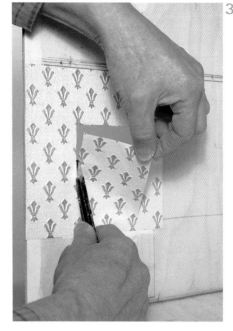

3 The wallpaper for the side walls should be cut to the right size and should overlap the back paper, which has turned the corner. Paper right over the window holes, then cut away the waste when the adhesive has dried. Then paper the partition walls.

ensure that the corner is well covered without a noticeable join. If you have rear or side windows, it is much simpler to paper right over the gaps and then cut out the window area with a craft knife when the paper has dried. It is a good idea to cut away a strip of paper all around the window opening so that the architrave has some wood to grip onto.

The choice of wallpaper for a doll's house is more important than for your own home. The whole house will be seen at once, so the colours should blend together to give an attractive overall appearance. Make sure that any patterns are small and in keeping with the 1:12 scale.

The way you decorate the large front doors is a matter of personal choice. Some people divide it up into sections with beading, then paper the appropriate divisions to match the individual rooms. Other people prefer to use a plain toning paper all over the inside.

Fit windows and their architraves when all the wallpapering is complete. Panelling is something that can be added at this stage if you wish. I always glaze the window behind a chimney breast before I add the ceiling. I also know from experience that trying to screw rings above the windows for curtain rods can be a problem.

Ceiling coving, skirting boards and the staircases are added after the house is finished.

Only one action can be explained at a time, but in practice they all dovetail into each other to become a single sequence. At the end of the book is an outline schedule for completing the downstairs decorating.

FINISHING INTERNAL DECORATION

1 Trim any surplus paper from the wall partitions.

2 Add the architraves around the door when you have papered the partition.

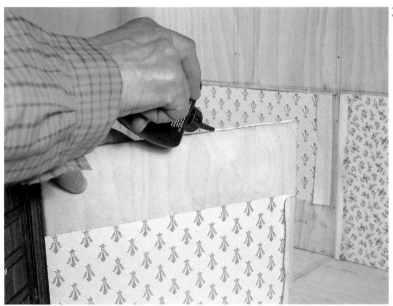

3 Run adhesive along the back and bottom edges of the partition.

4 Slide the partition into place and screw it to the back wall from the outside.

FINISHING INTERNAL DECORATION

5 Paste the bare corner between the back wall and partition.

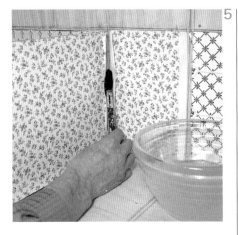

6 Add paste to the rear paper so that it comes around the corner and onto the side panel.

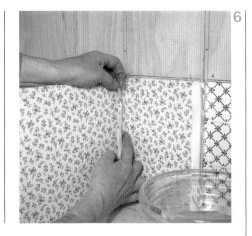

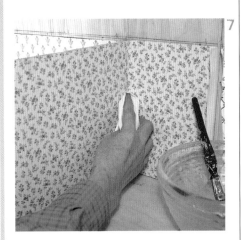

7 Stick the paper on the panel right into the corner.

8 Cut away a sliver of paper before adding the architraves to doors and windows.

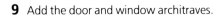

9 Add the door and window architraves.

10 Wall panelling can be made by gluing three different widths of narrow beading to 1/16 in (2 mm) ply. Stain all wood before gluing.

11 Glue the rear panel first, then butt the side panels into the corners.

12 The front side panel under the window butts up against the chimney breast. (Making the fireplace, windows and curtains are covered later in the book.)

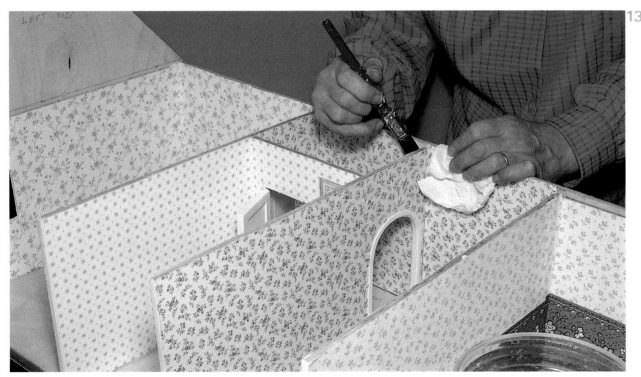

13 When all the decorating is finished you can screw and glue the ceiling of the first floor in place. The upstairs is decorated in the same way. Remember that the corridor behind the bathroom must be papered and the electrics and floor covering laid before the upper ceiling is fixed.

9
WIRING YOUR DOLL'S HOUSE

No two houses are the same, and each will need a different approach. The basic system is common to all buildings, and the explanation that follows will enable you to wire the doll's house described in this book.

Most professionals will tell you to hide the wiring behind the wallpaper. That is fine if you can guarantee that nothing will ever go wrong. I would strongly advise you to make your wiring concealed but accessible. The candle-shaped grain of wheat bulbs, for example, can be replaced only by removing their attached wires, and even if you use the larger pea bulbs, you need extra flex to give room for your fingers to unscrew a blown bulb from its holder. Bulbs also work loose and need screwing up. Remember you cannot wallpaper rooms with the lights in place.

When you are trying to decide how many lights you should install, think of your doll's house rooms as your own home and decide where and how many lights you would have in real life. Having decided this, you must have all the lights ready before you begin, because installing electrical wiring really is a chicken and egg problem.

Soldering is easy – you need only a few minutes to learn how to do it – but it opens up infinite possibilities and permutations for lighting. You will need to buy a reel of copper tape. Single strip will give you greater flexibility than the plastic-covered twin strip, and it is available from most hobby and craft shops. When it comes to the wire, the opposite is true – use a twin flex, which is neater than the single.

Think of your own home. You have a ring main circuit that starts and finishes at the fuse box. These wires are tapped at various places for

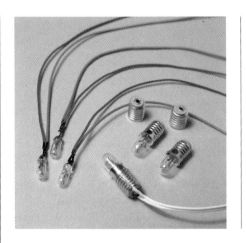

LEFT Grain of wheat bulbs (left) have the wires attached, and the whole unit has to be removed if the bulb blows. Pea bulbs (right) are more practical because you wire the holders and only the bulbs need changing. All bulbs are 12 volt.

BELOW There are dozens of everyday items that can be used for making miniature lamps.

WIRING INDIVIDUAL LIGHTS

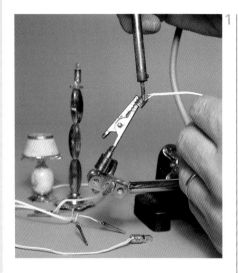

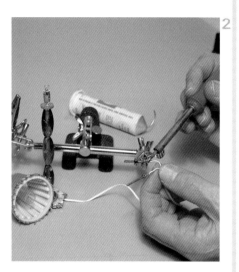

1 Solder one wire from the twin flex to the outside casing of the holder and the other to the centre rivet. Do not poke this wire through the rivet hole because it could cause a short if it touches the side of the bulb or inside the holder. A cheap gadget called "Helping Hand" (or "Third Hand") is extremely useful.

2 If you cannot obtain plugs and sockets, as a stop-gap you could try soldering the twin flex to slim, cut-down split pins, which can be pushed into brass tubing sockets so that they fit snugly.

lights or power points, each of which forms a secondary circuit. If one of them breaks and a light bulb or plug fuse blows, the ring main is not affected and all other lights and sockets remain operative. The wiring is said to be in parallel, and this is the system you should adopt in your doll's house.

Copper tape is your ring main and the transformer is your fuse box. All lights are then taken from as many points as you like on the circuit. Although it is called a circuit, you do not have to make a complete circle

RIGHT Two parallel strips of copper tape will be the equivalent to a household ring main, and you can take off it as many lights as you require. Nineteen ceiling lights were taken from one of the three circuits in the Lighting Shop.

with each length of copper tape. Two parallel, open-ended strips of copper are all that you need. The circuit is completed when you wire a bulb onto these strips. You can have as many circuits as you like and feed any number of lights off each.

All the wires destined for the transformer will come together, preferably at the rear of your house, and then into a cheap plastic connector block, which will link one common exit wire to the transformer.

LAYING A CIRCUIT

The simplest method of installing a circuit is to lay all your wiring under a removable floor covering.

Drill holes in the floors at the points from which you want to hang ceiling lights in the room below. This is another job which could have been done before you assembled the house.

Lay two strips of copper tape across the floor area. You can just bend it around corners and press hard, but if you want to add twin strips directed at right angles, they have to be soldered, and if two strips cross you must cover the lower strip with insulating tape to avoid a short circuit. Some miniaturists use brass pins to join two pieces of tape, but while you are soldering other wires it is just as easy to use that.

Thread the light flex with its bulb and holder through the shade, through the ceiling rose and then through the drilled holes. Solder the ends to the nearest point on the copper circuit. Make sure that the wires are long enough for you to pull them down from below if you need to change a blown bulb or to raise the shade to grip the holder.

You can also solder the wires for plug sockets and red bulbs for the fires. Try to stagger all the connections so that the paired wires are not likely to touch and cause a short circuit.

LAYING CIRCUITS ON THE FIRST FLOOR

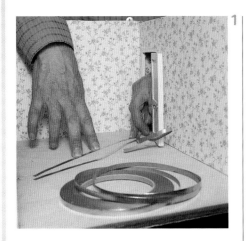

1 For the upstairs, lay two strips of copper tape across the room and guide them out into the corridor behind the bathroom.

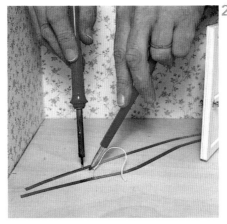

2 You will solder wires from one of the lounge ceiling lights and two fires and one bedside lamp onto this bedroom circuit.

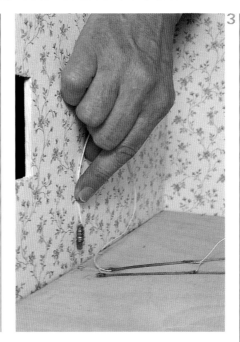

3 The lounge fire bulb has been dropped down the chimney to the open fire grate. The bedroom fire bulb shown here will be pushed through a hole on the far side of the chimney breast at floor level.

4 The completed bedroom fireplace.

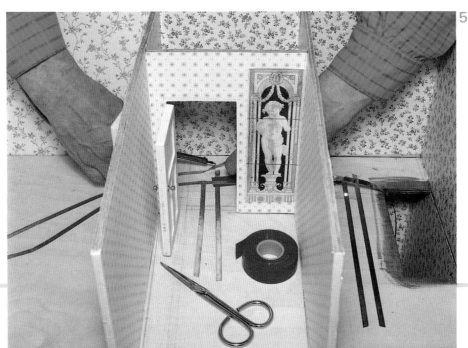

5 The landing circuit with a hall light from below, links up in the corridor with the bathroom, which takes the second lounge light. The flex leaves the house in the corner behind the stairwell. The right bedroom has its own circuit, with a wire leaving by the rear wall.

DOWNSTAIRS WIRING

1 Drill two holes, one for each of the brass tubing plug sockets, near the floor in the lounge and bedroom above.

2 The two pairs of brass tubing protrude from the inside to the outside. Two copper strips link these, then run the full width of the house to the external chimney flue behind the kitchen.

Place insulating tape over the soldered joints to stop the ceiling lights dropping lower into the room and to prevent the wires snagging when the floor covering is laid into place.

Think carefully before you install any wall lights. You could bring the wires down the wall after papering and hide them behind some furniture; they would be linked into the circuit on that same floor. Another possibility is to drill holes in the side walls and direct the wires outside where they can be disguised by painting, or laid under the edges of wall trim or between brick courses, or brought down external chimney flues. The wires are so fine that they will not be too obtrusive. Whatever you choose to do, remember to make them accessible, especially as most commercial wall lights have grain of wheat bulbs.

Fire lights can be dropped down hollow chimney breasts but a more favoured method is to drill a hole in the far side of the fireplace at floor level and poke the bulb through. If you adopt this method of lighting you can always add or move lights around when the house is finished. For example, you might need to move a bedroom light to one side to accommodate a four-poster bed. You could even drill this extra hole right at the outset to give you greater freedom in the furnishing.

Because the bathroom in this house has no side doors, you cannot lay one copper circuit right across the house. Instead you will need two separate circuits – one for the lounge/dining room and hall and one for the kitchen. You can also solder wires for the upstairs and downstairs fires onto these circuits. If you cannot buy plug sockets for any reason, brass tubing can be used. Take it back through the rear wall and use split pins as plugs to fit into the tube holes. You may decide to use copper tape on the outside rear wall rather than have several long, trailing wires.

You will need a pair of wires from each of the two circuits to poke through holes drilled near the floor on the back wall together with holes for wires from the downstairs lamp and cooker.

UPSTAIRS LIGHTING

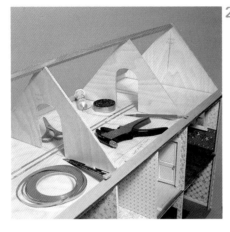

1 When the upper floor is complete prepare your lights and glue and screw in the ceiling.

2 Lay two strips of copper tape the full length of the roof floor. Solder onto these all the flex from the ceiling lights below.

3 The flex that is soldered to the ends of this loft circuit will drop down the outside rear wall.

4 A beam in the apex of each loft room rests on a pair of brackets. Wires from the three lights run along the top of the beams from room to room

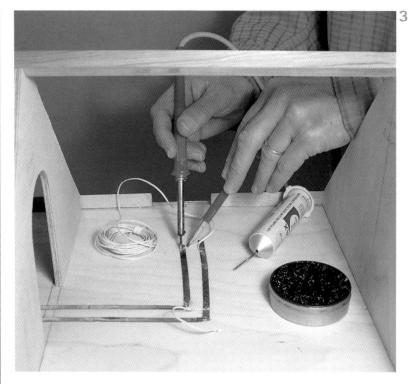

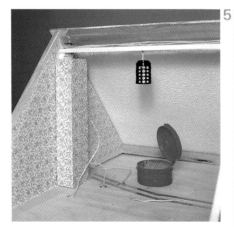

5 The three wires are held behind the chimney breast with doll's house wax and soldered onto the floor circuit.

For the upstairs lighting you can lay two strips of copper the full length of the roof space through the arched doorways. Wires from ceiling lights for the loft run along the top of beams in the apex. These beams rest on small brackets, but they are not fixed so they will always be removable. The three wires are guided down behind the chimney breast and soldered into the circuit on the floor.

TO THE TRANSFORMER

Now that the house is fully wired, the various circuits have to be connected to the mains through a transformer. Try to drill exit holes at the same point on each floor so that the wires can be hidden under one removable drain pipe or false flue.

Connector blocks come in plastic strips with pairs of screws along the length. Buy the smaller of the two sizes sold. They can be cut into multiples of four screws in a square, which for convenience I will refer to as one unit.

If you have no more than three pairs of wires leading from your circuits, the connection is simple. Separate the wires on each twin flex and, taking one wire from each, twist and solder them together. Do the same with the other three. Now you have two bundles of wire so you can screw them into the connector on one of the sides of a single unit. On the far side of the block, feed in another pair of wires a little thicker than the twin doll's house flex and only 3–4 in (7.5–10 cm) long.

This is soldered to the underside of a speaker terminal plate, which has red and black levers – these are obtainable from any good electronics or hi-fi shop. If you make a small box around the plate you can fix it to the back of your house with double-sided tape, Blu-tack or screws so that you can always take it off if necessary. All you have to do now is to flick the levers and pop in the two wires that lead from the transformer.

If you have more than three circuit wires from the doll's house you will need more than one connector unit, which is somewhat complicated to wire. Study the photograph carefully, but if you have any doubts, ask for professional advice.

TRANSFORMERS

A transformer will reduce the high voltage household current to a safe 12 volts for your miniature circuit. This low voltage cannot harm you if you touch it. *The transformer is one piece of equipment on which you should not skimp on cost.* It has to be serviceable and, above all, reliable. Look for one that has a casing with a grill to disperse heat. The cheapest versions are enclosed and usually have thin wires and a minimum iron core, which becomes red hot after a short run. Remember, too, that 12 volt DC (direct current) is more reliable than AC (alternating current), which tends to fluctuate upwards. Some transformers have 12 volt DC and 16 volt AC, so be careful if you want long-life bulbs. Make sure, of course, that you have 12 volt bulbs.

You must be absolutely certain that the transformer has a cut-out button, which is a built-in fuse that will save your house from bursting into flames if things go wrong. I once used an old model railway transformer, in which, unknown to me, the cut-out failed when I accidentally had a crossed wire. In barely two seconds my lounge filled with smoke and I had to rewire all 36 bulbs in the doll's house. False economy can be dangerous and costly.

Look out for a transformer with a variable speed, which works on the same principle as a household dimmer switch. It will prolong bulb life and gives more realistic period lighting.

I use a large, 4 amp transformer because it is necessary for a modeller's power drill and also because I can plug three houses in a row into it. This project house has 20 bulbs, so I would suggest that you use a 1½ amp transformer as minimum.

CONNECTING WIRING TO A TRANSFORMER

1 All the various circuits are linked into the copper tape circuit on the rear wall. Take off a pair of wires to the speaker terminal plate with its red and black levers. You will attach your transformer wires into this.

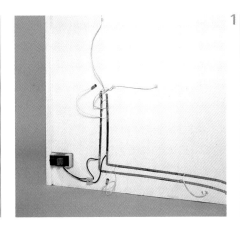

2 If you have many wires from a number of circuits you will need a long connector block, which should be wired as shown here.

3 An external chimney flue can be made from pieces of scrap wood because it will be either painted or bricked. It is a useful way to house the wiring.

4 The chimney flue can be attached to the wall with hooks and rings so that it is always possible to gain access to the lighting circuits.

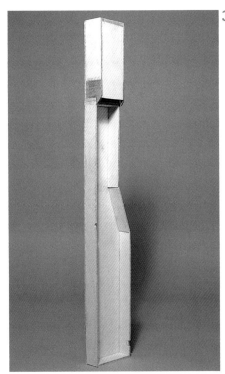

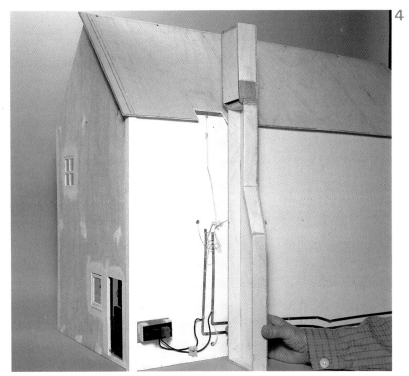

10
WINDOWS

Look around your town and out in the country and you will see a great variety of windows. Choose a style that suits the house you are building and study how the framework is built up. Notice especially which pieces of wood are longest and in which direction they are fixed. Windows usually resemble doors, with the long, vertical strips and the shorter cross-bars between. Look at the pattern of the glazing bars. Notice whether the windows are leaded or contain plain sheet glass.

Until you are an experienced woodworker you would be unwise to attempt sash windows. If you buy these ready made, remember that you cannot paint them because they are made so accurately that the sliding/opening movement has no spare room at all. You can of course, stain them. A casement window for the kitchen in this project house can be simply made using the pin method as described in the door section (see page 44).

If you decide to have non-opening windows, start by making an accurate template. Place a piece of card behind the hole, using a book or something similar to keep the card flat. Draw around the window hole and cut out this shape. This is yet another job that could have been done before you assembled your house and while the wood was lying flat on your workbench. Place this card on the acrylic sheet or perspex and draw around it. Cover the clear material with a piece of fine paper to prevent it from getting scratched, sticking it on with any washable paper glue.

Cut out the acrylic and test to see if it fits the hole reasonably accurately. Thin acrylic sheet can be cut with scissors or a knife. If you use perspex you will need either a fine-toothed saw or a sharp craft knife,

ABOVE An effective leaded window can be made by scoring the perspex with a sharp steel scriber.

ABOVE Windows of differing size and shape will need a template for each.

and it can be shaved down with coarse sandpaper or by scraping the knife along the edge.

For all your windows you will need many lengths of narrow, thin, well-sanded, strips of wood, which have to be painted or stained on both sides before they are cut. This is a time-consuming job, but it saves you getting splashes of paint on your windows. You may prefer to use white plastic strips.

CASEMENT WINDOWS

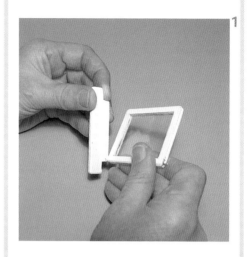

1 Make an opening casement window with pin hinges as described under the door section (see page 44).

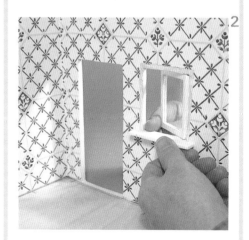

2 The upper pin is pushed into a hole in the top frame. The lower pin sits in a hole in the sill, which is glued to the frame.

MAKING A BAY WINDOW

1 These are the parts you will need to construct the bay window. The exact scale and size will depend on your personal taste and the size of your house.

2 It is basically a simple box shape.

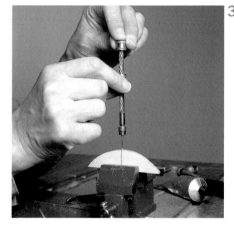

4 Pin a strip of ¹⁄₃₂ in (1 mm) ply into this hole.

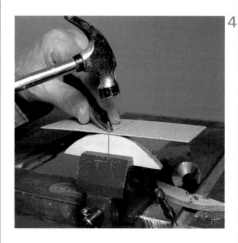

3 Pre-drill a small pin hole in the top centre of the curved section.

5 Drill and pin the ply at intervals all round the curved top.

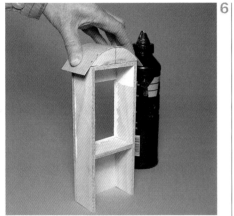

6 Glue it to the box frame.

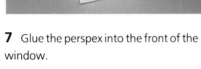

7 Glue the perspex into the front of the window.

8 Make a wooden frame, inserting the vertical strips first, then the horizontal ones and finally the glazing bars.

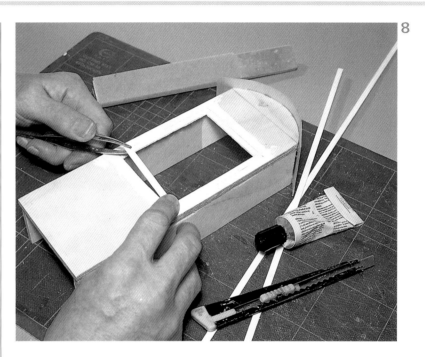

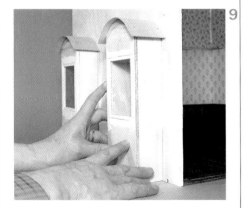

9 The whole bay unit is glued to the outer wall so that the inner ply edges are flush with the hole in the wall.

10 On the inside set in the windowsill, cut to fit.

11 The side walls should be put in place after the sill.

12 Finally, position the window architraves.

Because the acrylic sheet is thin and flexible, give the cut-out shape a border of strip wood, remembering to glue the vertical pieces first. Use a clear spirit-based glue. This is a messy job and needs careful application to avoid causing damaging smudges. Test that it fits tightly in the window hole and trim it down if necessary. Glue it in place. Add another frame to the inside, pressing it hard against the wood of the house so that any gaps on the outside will be filled in. Now you can add the glazing bars in your chosen pattern on both sides.

Perspex is thick enough to be glued directly in place, so you can add the frame while it is *in situ,* and the beading will fill in any gaps automatically.

Perspex can also be used to give the effect of a leaded window. A simple method is to make a diamond pattern on a sheet of paper and lay the perspex shape on top. Following the lines, score the surface with a sharp steel scriber on one side only. The reflection of the light in the grooves will give a good imitation of leading.

Unless you are a master-craftsman or have a die-cast machine, all your windows will vary slightly, and you will have to make a template for each individual one. The windows on each floor may be a different shape, varying from long or wide in the main rooms, to square near the top of the house.

DORMER WINDOWS

Dormer windows may at first seem very complicated. However, once you have grasped the mathematics they will not seem quite such a problem.

The actual opening in the roof will probably be 3 × 3 in (7.5 × 7.5 cm), but this is not the size of the glass. Draw a line 3 in (7.5 cm) long on a piece of card and another at right angles from the centre of this line. The 3 in (7.5 cm) line is the base of your triangle. Now move the right-angled set square up and down the centre line until the sides touch the outer

ABOVE Dormer windows add an interesting feature to a house.

points of the base line; draw around the right angle. This triangle of card forms a template for the sides of your dormer. When the longer base is held against the opening in the roof, the window will look upright at the front.

Cut two of these triangles in wood and add a roof that is the width of your required window. Draw a line around the inside and cut out this roof area so that the two walls can be glued to the wood, flush with the hole in the roof. The dormer is, in effect, another small box that is stuck to the roof. The flat lid of a dormer overhangs the walls. If the top is gabled, the lid must be flush so that the gables can overhang. Glaze the front as you would any other window.

DORMER WINDOWS

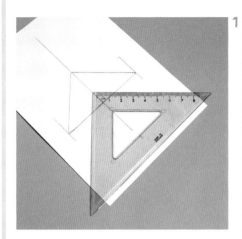

1 Take the width of the hole you require in the roof. Draw a line in the centre at right angles to it. Move a set square point up this line until the sides touch each end of the line. This is the template for the walls of your dormer window.

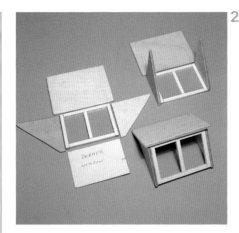

2 The component parts of the dormer window and the order of assembly.

3 Before you add the top of the window, draw around the inside to determine the area that is to be cut away in the roof.

4 The roofing material is added after the window is fixed. Here textured wallpaper has been used which will be painted with dark grey paint, to create the effect of a tarred roof.

5 The sides can then be bricked or painted and a windowsill added.

11
THE ROOF

The roof of your doll's house will be governed by the shape of your highest wall; in this case, the side panels are the highest. If you opt for attic rooms or merely loft storage space you will have direct access to the bedroom lighting. If you decide to have a sealed roof space, you can run the upstairs light flex along a groove in beams that are held against the ceiling with doll's house wax.

Because this project has attic rooms, the bedroom lighting circuit can run along the floor of the roof area. The attic ceiling light wires are laid across beams held in the apex of the roof on brackets (see page 55).

The wood used for the roof is ⅛ in (4 mm) because it will be strengthened with tiles, but it is a good idea to increase the width of the side walls on which it will be resting by adding another full section, which can be clamped tight against the original outer wall.

Cut a length of ½ in (12 mm) square strip beading to fit exactly between the two peaks, placing it with a corner edge uppermost. Glue and screw this ridgepole into place. Also glue strips of triangle wood along the floor on both edges of the roof. Before gluing the rear beading, cut out a section where your lighting wires will leave the house. If you

FIXING THE BACK OF THE ROOF

1 Strengthen the gable ends with a lining. This also gives ½ in (12 mm) sloping walls to support the roof.

2 A strip of ½ in (12 mm) beading between the gable ends forms a ridgepole. Also add triangle beading between the gables at floor level. Remember to leave a gap for your exit wires which will drop down the outside rear wall. The rear slope of the roof is fixed first. Paper it if you want attic rooms. Room dividers help to support the panel.

LEFT The opening front is often hinged to the ridgepole as in this house.

have an external chimney flue on the rear of the house, for example, position the gap so that the wires can run down the flue.

Because this project house is nearly 3 ft (90 cm) wide, the roof has been given additional support with two central dividers. If you are making rooms in the roof space, you may like to have doors in the partitions instead of arches.

The rear slope of the roof should be cut and fixed first so that it overlaps the back and side walls to form eaves.

Because the kitchen and the right bedroom windows are staggered,

MAKING A ROOF OPENING

1 One method is to fix two strips of wood to the top and bottom of the front area and to make a centre panel that rests in the opening like a box lid.

4 You could add a shelf to the front wall as an attractive feature. A false top to the stairs can be positioned in the roof over the corridor behind the bathroom.

2 The inside beading to hold the centre panel of the roof in place need not be as thick as this – I could not buy small beading at the time. Fill in the gap behind the dormer window with a sill.

3 The attic will look more homely if you add walls to the front and back, to square off the rooms.

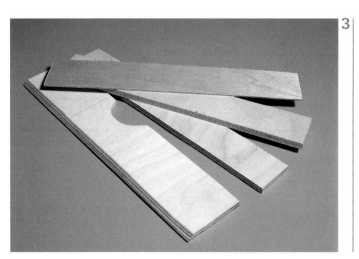

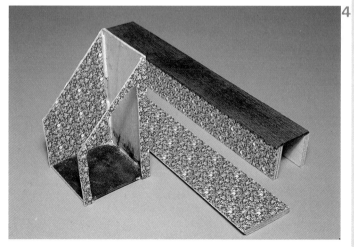

room fires will have to be located on the rear wall. A chimney flue can be made to cover the main electrics and will therefore have to be removable (see page 57). It is again a basic box shape. Remember to cut out a section in the rear roof panel where the chimney flue will slot into the roof. Glue and screw the panel in place.

Before you fix the second roof section you have to consider the eaves, which will impede the main house opening. This problem can be overcome by adding a strip of wood outside the front edge of the house so that the opening doors clear the lower edge of the roof. Do not let your overhang be too deep.

If you were able to make the peak of the roof at an angle of 45 degrees the front half will sit neatly over the rear section. You would, of course, have to cut the front area ⅛ in (4 mm) deeper than the rear section to allow for the overlap. Do not worry if the peak where the two halves of the roof meet is not perfect, because the join will be hidden by hollow triangle wooden ridge tiles. Use double-sided tape to hold the roof sections temporarily in place while you position the screw holes.

If your roof space is to open you have various options. First, you could hinge the front section along the ridgepole. Alternatively, you could glue and screw strips of beading around the underside of the roof in such a way that they sit snugly inside the house frame like a box lid. Another possibility is to fix two chimneys to the upper edge so the slope is angled to hook over the ridge.

One of the easiest ways to make a roof opening is to add a strip of wood to the ridge area and another at the eaves – pieces around 2 in (5 cm) deep will do. Fix some beading around the inside of the centre section of the roof so that the front opening fits into the space like a box lid. This removable section will need to be fitted with dormer windows if you are having attic rooms.

To make the attic space look like rooms, cut strips 2 in (5 cm) wide to

BELOW The attic rooms are complete apart from the floor covering.

stand at the back from the floor to roof and two similar strips for the front. A shelf over the front pieces gives an added feature for ornaments. Cut out a piece from the rear mini wall for the wire to pass through to the outside. The hole can be hidden by furniture later. Remember the chimney breast, which runs up from the left wall fireplaces on the floors below. Dismantle the parts, and paper the rooms before you glue it in place. The last feature to add is the box, to act as a false top for the stairs. As long as you position it realistically over the corridor behind the bathroom, the viewer will imagine that you have an unseen spiral staircase leading up to the attic!

12
THE FRONT-OPENING DOORS

LEFT The Tudor hall has a third door for the centre section.

The front of your doll's house is the feature that distinguishes it from every other.

There are a number of ways of tackling the opening. Do you want one complete, removable front or do you prefer two opening, hinged doors? Would you like to add an extension to one side like an extra room? Have you designed a high centre gable or a gable to one side? Sliding doors are another option.

If you have opted for a long veranda or any other elaborate feature that would be spoiled by cutting at any point, then one single, removable front is ideal. The drawback is that you always have to find somewhere to stand it when you open up the house. The front of the tythe barn, for example, is one piece.

Two long, opening, hinged doors are more traditional. The division between the two is usually made so that the hall/landing and one upstairs and one downstairs rooms are on one door while the remaining two rooms form a slimmer door. The centre section will be attached to the

LEFT Two long opening doors are more traditional. In this manor the mansard roof and the front porch/garden are separate units.

half that has less weight or width. These long doors are practical, and they sweep the eye to the interior as they open.

If you want an L-shaped front extension, you can simply make a small house as you would make a box and attach it to the front, hinged to the outside wall edge. Because of the extra weight, you have to keep this as one separate door, and the hall would be linked to the other half. The farmhouse has such an extension, which increases the size of the rooms and also adds an interesting feature when the house is open.

You might like to extend the lower part of the flat half to come level with the room extension by adding a shop front or an open veranda. The popular Honeychurch Victorian doll's house shop has this kind of frontage.

A flat but high-sided gable would again form one of the doors on its own. Depending on its height, you would have to add a roof that fitted the slope of the main roof, which is not an easy job for a beginner. Practise with a dormer window in the roof to learn the principle.

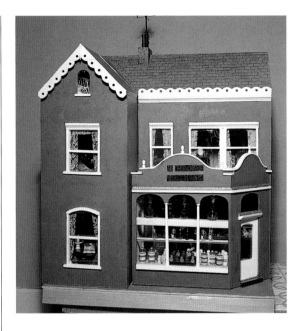

ABOVE Both sides of the popular Honeychurch Victorian shop are extended at the front.

ABOVE The weight of the L-shaped room extension means that it has to be made as a separate door.

RIGHT An open extension adds an interesting feature to a house.

RIGHT This was an original, rather plain house front.

FAR RIGHT By turning it round and remaking the gable end into an opening door, then adding extensions on either side, a completely different aspect was achieved. The upper gable section is removable for access to the wiring only – that is, it is not a usable room. The arcade and kitchen at the sides are separate units, and the whole building can be transported in three easily disassembled sections. One day the lower half will have herringbone brick inlay.

RIGHT The front of the Queen Anne house is hinged on one side only but is divided into two halves horizontally.

ABOVE The San Francisco house front caused problems because of its complexity and so the house actually opens at the rear.

RIGHT An elaborate front of the kind on this tythe barn does not lend itself to two opening doors. It has to be removed in one piece.

If you choose sliding doors you will require a router to make a deep groove, or you can add channelling with plastic strip. Alternatively glue two pieces of strip wood to make a groove. The drawbacks are that all channelling is visible, gathers dust and eventually snaps. It also means you must have a perfectly flat front with no side extension on the eaves. Another major problem is that curtains and other features on the inside will jam the smooth running, and the little front door has to be hinged to open outwards if you want it to stay intact.

Whichever style you choose, cut the wood to size first then cut out the door and window openings. Do not use thin wood for this frontage, because it is weakened when the door opening is cut away. Even ¼ in (6 mm) is liable to warp, especially if you use a water-based glue, paint or wallpaper paste. You can overcome this by clamping the whole section to a flat bench and sizing it with either wallpaper paste or a water-based primer paint. Leave it clamped until the wood is thoroughly dry.

The small front door is made in a similar way to the internal room doors and in any style you choose. Add the hinges while you still have the big doors on the bench.

A door fitting that is often used for shops is also acceptable for some houses. Cut it slightly larger than the opening so that it sits behind the frame. Lay your hinges flat on the inside surface and across to a strip of the same wood. This strip is then glued and/or pinned to the inside wall.

The big hinges need a good grip with longer screws because of the extra wear and tear of the constant opening and knocking. Piano hinges are best because you do not need to recess the wood. Screw them to the doors first and mark up the position of screw holes on the front wall edges. If you feel it is necessary, insert plugs of dowel in the side walls as described on pages 22–3.

MAKING THE FRONT OPENING

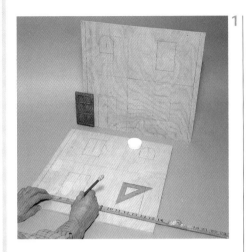

1 Cut out the large front doors and draw in the windows and front door.

2 Cut out the windows and door, then check that this style is your final choice.

3 Make the front door in the same way as the internal doors. Decide on the style of the surrounds and make them with whatever materials you can acquire.

4 Piano hinges are by far the best type for the heavy front opening. Divide the inside with beading to correspond to the layout of the rooms.

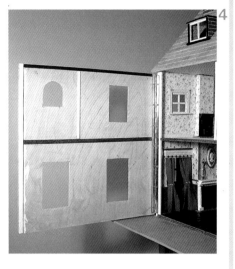

5 Paper the inside to match the rooms or use a plain paper throughout.

6 Add the strip of beading under the eaves to fill the gap above the doors.

13
FINISHING THE INTERIOR

FLOOR COVERINGS

Because the wiring is on the floors, the floor covering has to be removable so that you have access to the electrics. You may perhaps select an all-over carpet, or possibly you might prefer patterned "lino" paper stuck to a piece of soft card. Whatever you use, it can usually be held down with double-sided tape, which can be stuck to the floors in the areas between the copper tape.

An effective method is to stain and polish strips of wood and, using plenty of white wood glue, stick them to a close-weave fabric such as curtain lining. You can roll up the floors as you would a roll-top desk so that they can be squeezed into the rooms and then spread out around the various fittings, such as fireplaces.

Cut the flooring to size after the skirting boards have been fitted.

ABOVE Suitably grained wallpaper can make an acceptable wooden floor when it is stained.

LEFT Vinyl floor tiles also have their uses. If the surface is too rough, fill it in with wall filler. Cut the tile into strips, then into tile or paving slabs. Pick them up at random and glue them to the floor.

A FLEXIBLE WOODEN FLOOR

1 Glue strips of wood stained to your chosen colour to close-weave material to make a flexible boarded floor.

2 When it is cut to size, the floor can be rolled up, inserted into a room, then spread out neatly around fittings like fireplaces.

3 If the sheet is pressed down onto double-sided tape laid between the wiring, it can be removed if necessary.

FIREPLACES

When it comes to selecting a fireplace, your best plan is to study photographs and to see what materials you can acquire to build up the fire surround. If you have opted for external chimney flues, you will have to stick a box to the outside wall to cover the hole you cut away. Inside the room you will need only a fire surround. Fireplaces must be authentic, so take care that you do not position them under or over a window in another room. They must have a common flue right up the house.

Corner fireplaces take up less room, but recesses offer more opportunities for interesting furniture.

If you have an internal fire, you need to stick a wallpapered chimney breast to the room wall, with the fireplace and surround built into the lower one-third of the chimney breast. For both purposes 1/16 in (2 mm) ply or balsa wood is light and practical.

When it comes to decorating the fire surround, you can use a variety of oddments, such as fans, bracelet links, plastic flowers and leaves, jewellery bits, fancy cord and ribbons. Almost anything can be used. When painted they look like plaster carvings.

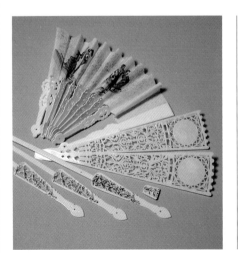

LEFT Plastic fans have a wide variety of uses. The filigree carving can be cut and used almost anywhere including for the decoration of a fire surround. You could also use them for garden furniture and iron staircases.

RIGHT The basic internal chimney breast can be made from any thin scrap wood. For the bedroom fires you could use model railway plastic brick sheets, the waste from model kits and shelf brackets cut from shaped strips of wood.

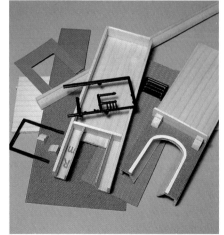

ABOVE An external firegrate is merely a thin ply box over a hole in the wall. The advantages are that the fire surround can be laid flat against the wall to save space in a small room and you have an exit line for wiring down the flue. The disadvantages are that recesses around an internal fireplace can add interest to a square room and bricking is a long, tedious process.

MAKING A FIREPLACE

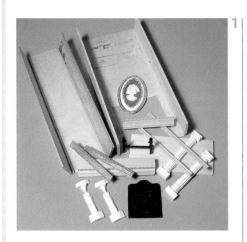

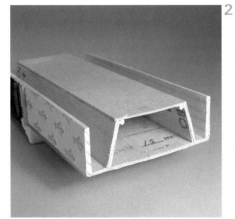

2 If you need to drop the light bulb down a hollow flue into the main grate, make the chimney breast in two parts.

3 The front of the fireplace before decoration.

1 For the main room fireplace you can use a mixture of oddments and shelf and pillars from a doll's house specialist. The caryatids came from a small spirit bottle and the cameo was a broken brooch – both bought on junk stalls. The fireback is merely a shaped thin ply with a smooth, unravelled strand of string for the surround and jewellery oddments for decoration.

4 The fireplace in position. The cameo is supported with doll's house wax, so it can be replaced with a mirror or picture if you wish. The fire surround can be enhanced by any strip of decorative beading.

MAKING CURTAINS WITH A PELMET

2 This small free sample of wallpaper was intended for the chimney breast, but the pattern was too big. The border though, was ideal for the pelmet, which was made from plywood and ¼ in (6 mm) beading.

3 Pre-drill tiny holes in the architrave for screw rings to take the curtain rods.

1 Authentic curtain rods, rings and end caps can be expensive and are not readily available. Necklace clasps are a good substitute for the rings, and they can be threaded on brass rod with plastic tubing for end caps.

4 The pelmet is held in place with doll's house wax so that the curtains are accessible if you ever want to change them. Always dress the window that is behind a chimney breast before you add the ceiling.

MAKING A BLIND

1 Blinds can be made by soaking material in wallpaper paste. Allow it to dry and then press, before sticking to a brass rod.

2 Add a piece of cord and a bead or seed for the blind pull.

CURTAINS

Curtains should be made of thin material, and if patterned, make sure it is in scale. You may want to change your curtains when you redecorate the house in years to come, so make them removable. Spring necklace clasps make good curtain rings: sew the loops to the material and run the wider rings on brass rods. Snippets of plastic tubing will make rod caps. Hold pelmets in place with doll's house wax so they can be taken off to allow you to reach the curtains.

Blinds can be made from any material that has been stiffened by soaking in wallpaper paste and glued to rods. Only the dedicated make blinds that roll down!

THE STAIRCASE

Tape the upper stair treads to the cardboard mock room in the position it will occupy in the house. Banisters are best purchased ready made, but if you cannot obtain these, they can be made with dowling and small blocks of wood. This is a very fiddly and frustrating process and perhaps not ideal for the beginner, so you may decide to opt for solid panels which are an easier alternative.

To be realistic, the banisters should sit in the middle of the tread on the outer edge of stairs that are made with stringers, treads and risers. In practice, you need to be a master craftsman to keep them upright and firmly fixed. If this is your first doll's house, glue them not only to the stair treads but also further back so that they are supported by the risers. This method makes them less fragile and easier to fix. Because the staircase is supported on the cardboard, the banisters can be glued in a true upright position.

As you near the top of the stairs, the banisters will be taller than the ceiling. You can either cut them progressively shorter or add a solid piece of ply, cut to fit this space.

If you used triangle wood for stairs, the length of ply added to the outside edge should, in theory, be more solid and the banisters would sit on the top. In practice, you will find it more practical to glue the banisters in the angles between the treads, risers and outer support. This may not be strictly authentic, but it is easier for the inexperienced.

Newel posts for the top and bottom of the stairs can be bought ready-made or they can be carved out of wood. A simple method is to build them from square wood, dowel and beads. To make them stronger, drill holes through the component parts and force a length of brass rod through them.

The handrail is always a problem. Again, it is possible to buy ready-made ones or you can make something serviceable yourself. Cord glued to the top of each banister is often used, stiffened with paint or glue. Brass or plastic channelling is available in most hobby shops.

You will need to have a rail around the stairwell on the upper landing. You can use solid panels between the newel posts or make a surround of banisters. These are stuck to a thin strip of wood, fitted on the floor

ABOVE An enclosed staircase means that you will not need banisters. It is useful, too, for making a false staircase. In the Manor, the space under these stairs was used to extend a tiny bathroom.

RIGHT A boxed upper stairwell can be used to make a bedroom cupboard as in this room.

FINISHING A STAIRCASE

1 Use the mock cardboard hall to keep the glued banisters in an upright position.

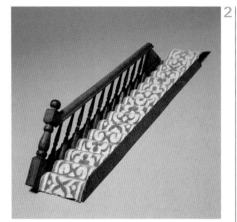

2 The staircase needs a newel post at the foot of the stairs and three for the stairwell surround above. Stick carpeting to the staircase and glue brass rods in the angles. A triangular piece of wood will fill the gap near the ceiling.

3 Do not secure a staircase until the hall or the room is complete.

between the newel posts and the handrail on top. Stair rods can be cut from brass rods and glued into the angles between treads and risers.

Do not secure any staircase permanently into your house until you have decorated and carpeted the hallways.

A simple method of fixing stairs is to have them supported not only by the room divider wall but also by another ceiling-height wall, which can be used in place of banisters. This is a useful device when staircases do not go anywhere. A solid surrounding wall allows you to partition off a stairwell, and you can make a cupboard over the stairs for added

interest. You could, for example, use the space under a false staircase to extend a tiny bathroom.

In the doll's house made as a project here, part of a bedroom has been used to create a bathroom. It would have been possible to move the bathroom wall right up to the staircase and so to retain a larger bedroom. However, the landing area is more useful for a linen cupboard and for other furniture or toys.

14
FINISHING THE OUTSIDE

Once you have finished the interior, you should re-hinge the front opening. Many people merely paint the outer walls, but this has the effect of making them look more like toys than true miniature houses. It is possible to add a variety of features to create an authentic appearance. Outside features can also hide a multitude of sins! Remember, it's the finished product people see, not the mistakes made on the way.

The style you have devised for the interior will dictate how you decorate the outside. The walls can be covered by rendering made from an exterior strength proprietary filler or emulsion paint mixed with sand, and even painted sawdust looks effective. Weatherboarding (clapboard siding) is long strips of ¹⁄₁₆ in (2 mm) ply stuck to the walls with impact adhesive. Start at the bottom of the wall and slightly overlap each layer.

BRICKS

Much trial and error has shown that one of the best ways to make all brickwork is with F2 grade sandpaper. First, paint the surface wood to represent mortar. Then stick on the bricks individually with a clear spirit glue which dries quickly. Bricking is a long, tedious business, but using tweezers helps considerably.

A cutting gadget from pieces of scrap wood is perfect for cutting the strips to an even width without slicing your fingers. Paint and stipple the sandpaper and cut the strips first, then cut the brick lengths, using the width of a length of wood as a guide. Leave some strips uncut for the halves and odd shapes around the windows.

ABOVE An external-strength proprietary filler is usually used for cement rendering, as on this little shop. Paint and sand, paint and sawdust (powdered or in little curls) or embossed wallpaper can also be used.

WEATHERBOARDING THE EXTERIOR

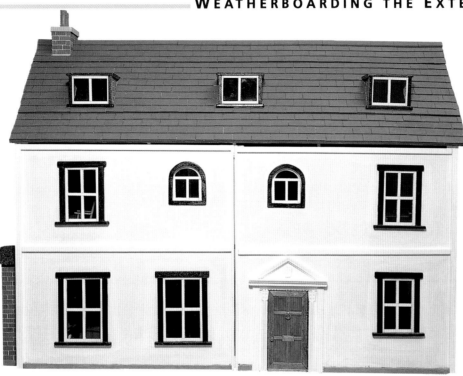

1 With only a base coat of paint, the house is ready for its outside decoration. The choice is unlimited: you could paint, cement render, brick, tile, weatherboard or add Tudor beams. You can use any combination for the upper and lower halves of the building. Other possibilities are to add shutters, a veranda, balconies, a porch, plain or gingerbread trim, a garden or even a street scene. In this case a weatherboard finish was chosen.

2 Start at the bottom, slightly overlapping each board. If you use strong contrasting colours, paint the contact tips of every strip, or you will end up on an endless round with a brush in each hand, one black, one white!

3 Cut around the windows. Beading around the brick and roof contacts gives a neat finish.

REALISTIC BRICKS

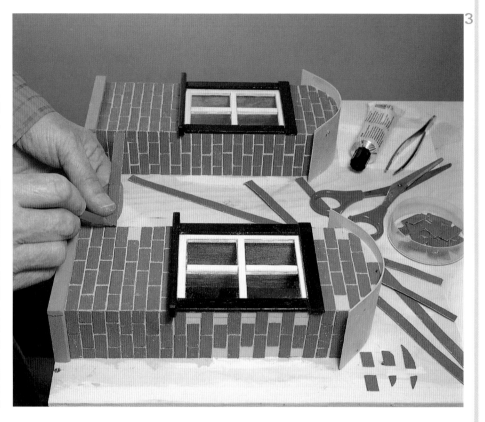

1 Paint and stipple sheet sandpaper to the shade you require. Make a cutting board from scrap wood. This will ensure the strips are an even width and keep your fingers away from the blade.

2 Cut the strips into bricks by using a strip of board ¾ in (2 cm) wide as a measure. Save some strips for the halves and odd shapes.

3 Paint the wall the colour of cement rendering, then glue the bricks onto the walls one at a time with spirit glue. You can brick an entire house, or just a section as I have done here.

The guide blocks on the cutting board are held in place with double-sided tape, so they can be replaced with wider pieces if, say, you want to cut large slabs for the kitchen floor. When the cutting groove grows too deep, it is not necessary to replace the board. Fill up the groove with wood glue or a glue and sawdust mix until it is flush with the surface.

If you would like to have red clay hanging wall tiles, use plain sandpaper and stick it to tiles of 1/16 in (2 mm) ply or scalloped shingles. Use impact adhesive to glue them to the wall and then paint all over.

THE ROOF

Do you want slate, clay tiles or stone slabs? Hobby shops sell grooved cedar shingles, but these are filmsy and are not easy to lay because they vary in thickness. They are available in straight or scalloped shapes. Shingles are also sold in a smooth wood, but these can easily be made from tongue depressors, obtained from your chemist. Use an impact adhesive because a water-based glue will cause them to warp.

To make your own roofing tiles you can either cut up lengths of

TILING A ROOF

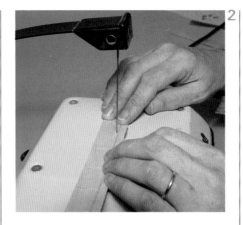

ABOVE Some samples of useful tiles (from the top): a row of commercial cedar tiles; 1/16 in (2 mm) ply and the scallop ends of tongue depressors; tiles covered with sandpaper to represent clay tiles; the reverse side of embossed wallpaper, glued to tiles for quarry stone slabs.

1 Use a scrap of wood as a measuring stick to divide a strip into equal tiles.

2 Cut along these lines, but only two-thirds of the way through.

3 Glue the strips to the roof so that the tiles overlap the lower row and also so that the divisions alternate by half a tile in each row.

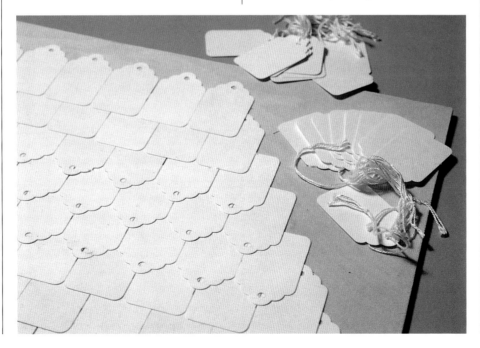

LEFT Price tags or plain card can be used as cheap roof tiles.

TILING A ROOF

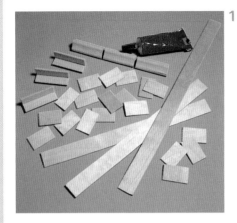

1 The tiles were made from ⅟₁₆ in (2 mm) ply, but curved right-angle beading was used for ridge tiles.

2 You should add a narrow strip beneath the lowest row in each of the three separate units of the front opening to keep the appearance of overlapping.

3 Cut the tiles around obstructions.

4 Paint the tiles in whatever colour you choose and neaten the hollow ends with cement filler.

⅟₁₆ in (2 mm) ply into individual pieces or simply cut the strips two-thirds of the way through and glue them onto the roof in their strips. The uncut portion will be hidden under the upper row.

Cross-cutting is another effective way of producing tiles, but it is more complicated and you will need a machine. Slice a length of square strip wood in the way you slice bread. These pieces have an attractive, grained effect.

Look out for different patterns of embossed white wallpaper. Choose a small, bubbly pattern and squash the lumps with a piece of wood. Stick plywood strips to the wallpaper and chop them into tile lengths. The reverse side of the wallpaper is often more realistic if you want to simulate stone slabs. This method can also be used to make paving stones.

Strips of thin card make cheap and effective tiles. Ordinary price tag labels can be used either way: a straight edge on one side, or turn them around to create a scalloped pattern, enhanced by the holes intended for the string.

Hollow triangle moulding cut into short lengths and butted together are ideal for ridge tiles across the peak.

Depending on the style of your house, plain or decorative barge-boards under the roof edges of gable-end walls give your roof a final touch of realism.

THATCH

There is something irresistibly nostalgic about thatch, but the problem is to find a material to work with that lends itself to the 1:12 scale and at the same time looks realistic.

One of the best materials is hay, although unravelled garden string is a good alternative and is considerably easier to apply – it is purely a matter of personal preference.

Whatever you use, you must thatch in the manner of real houses,

A THATCHED ROOF

2 While the hay is held in the clamp you have two hands for tying the bundle.

3 If your strip of wood is the correct length, you also have a measure to cut the bundles uniformly.

1 A simple gadget will help hold the loose hay in a narrow channel. Velcro stapled to the board and flap gives a quick clasp.

4 Use a non-drip contact adhesive and also sew the bundles to a painted plastic embroidery mesh.

RIGHT Thatch from unravelled string as used here is another alternative, but remember that you cannot have an opening roof if you thatch it.

stitching and/or gluing individual thumb-sized bundles to the roof. You will find it useful if you make a simple gadget that leaves both hands free for knotting. A thatched roof is practical only if your roof is a fixture with no opening.

BASEBOARD

Adding a baseboard means that there is less stress on your house when it is moved around, and it also prevents chipped corner walls. If you have external chimney flues or other extensions then a base is essential; it need not protrude more than 1–2 in (2.5–5 cm) around the bottom of the house.

You should use ¼ in (6 mm) or ⅓ in (9 mm) wood because the

corners in particular are likely to come in for some rough treatment. Draw around the outside of your house on the board and make another line ¼ in (6 mm) inside this outline. Drill holes in the centre between the lines and marry them with drill holes on the underside of the house. Remember to countersink the screws on the underside of the baseboard to avoid scratching your furniture.

You may have a problem opening the front of your house if the bottom of the doors catch on the baseboard. Either take off the hinged doors and shave them down a fraction, or glue a length of quality beading, ¼ in (6 mm) or less, all around the base of the house before you screw on your baseboard. This will give sufficient clearance for the opening front without looking obtrusive.

MAKING A BASEBOARD

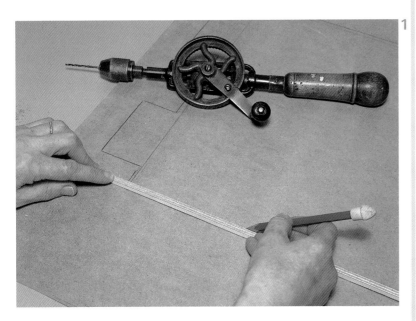

1 Draw round your house on the baseboard. Allow a small border all the way round, allowing more for any anticipated extras such as a veranda. Using a strip of ¼ in (6 mm) wood as a guide, draw a line ¼ in (6 mm) inside the outline. Drill holes between these lines to correspond to the lower wall ends of your house.

2 On the underside, countersink the screw holes. Glue and screw the board to the base of your house.

ABOVE A Bavarian chalet with plank shutters.

ABOVE Simple shutters can be made from thin ply with beading trim on one side only.

SHUTTERS

Simple shutters can be made from ¹⁄₁₆ in (2 mm) ply base, with beading added to one side only. The Bavarian plank shutters were made from ice lolly sticks.

CHIMNEYS

If you have an external chimney flue this automatically extends to a similar square shape. Chimneys that are on the roof centre have to sit astride the peak, and they should be fitted before you add the ridge tiles. You can also add a chimney halfway down the slope of the roof.

Always position the chimneys realistically in terms of the internal fireplaces, and remember that the number of chimney pots should correspond to the number of fires up each flue.

CHIMNEYS

1 Chimneys can be made any shape or size according to the style of your house. Use scrap wood to build them. This one was built to fit snugly over the roof of the house. Rough wood can be disguised by first painting with glue, then dipping it in sawdust. When dry, paint the "concrete".
2 Once the chimney has been finished to fit the style of the house, simple chimney pots can be made from dowel with trim. This pot was made from a filigree metal ribbon and dressmaking elastic. Because the pots are liable to be damaged while the house is being moved, make them removable with a peg of brass rod.

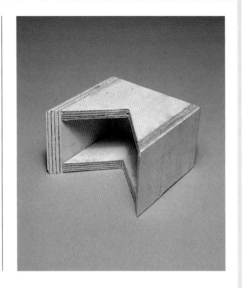

VERANDAS

You can make a veranda in any style or shape that you fancy and it can be as ornate or plain as you wish.

Although the aim is to be architecturally correct, purists will always find anomalies. If a house is pleasing to look at and appears to be authentic, you can feel happy. This is not a competition, but a satisfying and creative pastime that requires a variety of skills and techniques.

Now you have the completed house, ready for furniture and its people, although you will probably go on adding refinements for several months to come. Like your own home, no doll's house is ever really finished, but for the time being you can switch on the lights and admire your own dream home. The sense of achievement is exhilarating.

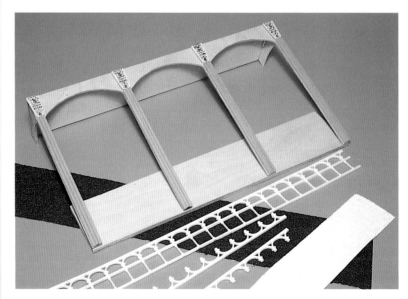

ABOVE The veranda was made up piecemeal from cut ply, wood beading and fancy trim, with ¼ in (6 mm) for the roof.

The base was glued then screwed to the house front before the wall panelling was glued inside.

RIGHT The addition of shutters gives the house a different look. The contrast of black and white is effective.

LEFT The veranda and the porch over the kitchen are further delicate details which can be added if you wish.

LEFT The house is now complete and waiting to be furnished.

15
A PROPOSED
WORK SCHEDULE

1 Make a scale plan on graph paper of all dimensions.

2 Transfer the plans to brown paper patterns in full scale (optional).

3 Draw each section onto ¼ in (6 mm) ply. Cut out and sandpaper.

4 Check you have the correct measurements and mark up positioning for the screw holes. Drill the holes.

5 Cut out windows and doors; cut out fireplaces if you will need them later.

6 Screw the left side and floor base together. Add the back panel and then the right side.

7 Check that the outer shell fits squarely together. Screw in the upper floors.

8 Mark the positions for the room dividers. Make the bathroom complex, which does not need grooving.

9 Stand back and consider whether the rooms are the sizes required. Think how and where you are going to lay the electric wires/tape. Do you want internal or external chimney flues? Do you want extensions? Is the house practical for the occupants living in the house? Is it too big for display?

10 Make the basic staircase. Do not add banisters yet. Hold it against the ceiling and mark the rear position for the stairwell.

11 Dismantle the house and make your alterations now. Cut out the stairwell. While the house is in sections, make templates for the inter-nal doors and windows. Drill holes for lights and plug socket outlets where they come on the main frame.

12 Reassemble the outer shell with glue and screws. Screw, but do not necessarily glue, the first ceiling. Slide in the room partitions but do not glue them. (At this stage I realized I hadn't hung the side kitchen door, so I had to make another door which fitted over the frame!)

13 Decorate and complete one floor at a time.

14 Touch up painting around the front edges of the house before paper-ing any room. Here is a check list for decorating the ground floor:

● Make the lounge chimney breast.

● Make the panelling to fit all round the room and either side of the fireplace.

● Paper the upper half of the room on the left and rear walls, leaving a small flap to overlap the right room divider wall.

● This room divider has its door hung first, then papered on both sides but only pasted to within ½ in (12 mm) of the corner. When it is glued in place, the overlap from the rear wall paper can be pasted around the corner to the divider and the third wall final ½ in (12 mm) pasted on top of the overlap right into the corner.

● Lay the wood block flooring.

● Glue in the panelling, starting with the back wall and butting the side panels up to these.

LEFT This simple thatched cottage has been enhanced by a country garden.

• Cut away the paper over the hole and assemble the windows. Fit screw rings and other fittings for the curtains.

• Glue in the chimney breast.

• Paper the rear of the hall and paste down the last ½ in (12 mm) on top of the back wall overlap.

• Hang the door on the kitchen divider and paper both sides, leaving the last ½ in (12 mm) unpasted as before.

• Finish the papering.

• Lay the floor covering last of all. Do not fix the staircase yet.

• Paper the rear wall of the kitchen, bringing the paper around the corner on both sides.

• Cut away the wallpaper over the door and window holes, plus a sliver all round to expose some of the wood.

• If you have made an overlap door, now is the time to fix it in place.

• Assemble the window and blind and lay the kitchen tiles.

15 When downstairs is complete, glue and screw your ceiling and move upstairs. If you have made my bathroom section then this will definitely have to be papered before its ceiling is added because you will never reach the passage behind the rear wall and yet it will be seen through the open doors. (Before decorating see step 17.)

16 Make and fit your internal chimney breasts on top of the wallpapered walls.

17 Assemble your downstairs lights and poke the wires through the ceiling. Hold them in place with adhesive tape or doll's house wax. Lay copper tape in such a way that it passes reasonably near the lights.

18 Finish decorating upstairs. Paint the rear outside wall before laying the tape. If the rear of your house will always stand against a wall, the wiring can be left open, otherwise you can hide it with a sheet of thin plywood lightly screwed in place as an over-panel. Alternatively, protect most of the wiring with a full-length chimney flue.

19 Cut the side panels for the left and two more for the centre. If this area is to be used for rooms, a boxed stairwell obviates the need to make a second staircase.

20 Glue and screw the side gable panels to the outer wall. Cut and screw in place the ridgepole and glue the triangle beading along each edge of the front and back upper walls. Cut the centre partitions to fit around these additions. Before gluing the rear triangle beading, cut a section out of it so that the lighting wires can pass through to the outside.

21 Solder all the upstairs lights to this circuit. Take off a wire to go through the slot in your triangle beading and down the outside wall to the baseboard, allowing a bit extra for fittings. Remember that the rear roof will be fixed, so if you ever have cause to change the outlet wire, you will have to be able to poke it through the beading slot, and this is a very tight roof angle for fingers. Leave the lighting link up to the mains for now and go back to finishing the house.

22 Fix the rear roof panel. Cut, prepare and add the front sections. Glue in place the chimney and tile the roof. Ridge tiles are fitted last.

23 Using the templates you made earlier, cut out the acrylic or perspex and make and fit all the windows you did not assemble during the decorating.

24 Glue in place the staircase with its banisters and newel posts. Make the upper landing stairwell surround. Do not glue this because the "room" is easier to furnish and it is less likely to be crushed if you can take it out.

25 Make and hang the front of the house and add the strip at the top under the eaves.

26 Go right round the house, filling in any gaps and sanding sharp corners. This smooth finishing is important if you are merely painting the outside. If you are adding bricks, rendering or weatherboarding, do it now.

27 Make the chimney flue to hide the wires. It must be removable. Wires from the downstairs plugs, if fitted, will run along the lower base.

28 Connect the circuit wires to the transformer and switch on!

ACKNOWLEDGEMENTS

Sincere thanks for the loan of their doll's houses are due to Barbara Herrington, Vivienne Kay, Clare Milligan, Anne Pollock and Stella Thomas. Thanks also to Valma and Paul Martin, who helped supply the building materials when needed.

INDEX

Page numbers in *italic* refer to illustration captions.

A

architrave 38, *43*, 44, 46, *47, 48*, 61

attic 19, 32, 64, 65, *66*, 67, *67*

    lighting in *55*, 56

B

banisters 33, 79–80, *81*, 94

barge board 86

baseboard 19, 88, *89*

basement 19

basic box *12*, 15, 24–7, *24, 25, 26, 27*

    roof for 26–7, *26*

bathroom *32*, 81, 92, 93

bay window 31, 60–1, *60, 61*

birch ply 22

blinds 79, *79*

box room 8, 13

brickwork 82, *84*, 94

C

ceiling 38, 39, 45, *46*, 49, 92, 93

chimney breast 31, 39, 46, 67, 76, *76, 77*, 92, 93, 94

chimney 67, 89, 90

clamp 23

clubs, craft 8

connector box 52, 56, *57*

copper tape 50, 51, 52, *52*, 56, 94

coving 39, 46

cupboard 45, 80, 81

D

decorating 38, 45–9, 92, 94

depth of house 19

designing 15, *16*, 19

doorknobs 38, 44, 45

doors, external 72, *73*

    to hang 42–4

    holes for *29*, 31, 92, 93

    internal 38, 40–4, *41*, 45, 92

    panelled 40–1, *41*

    size of 31

dormer window 62, *62*, 63, *63*, 67, 69

    size of 62

double hinged front 68, *69*

    horizontal *71*

double staircase 36, *37*

drill, types of 23

E

eaves 65, 67

electric circuit 50–2, *52, 53*, 54, *54*, 64, 94

exhibitions, craft 8

extension *10*, 31, 36, 68, 69, *70, 71*, 88

exterior finish 82–91, *82, 83*, 94

external door 72, 73

external flue *57*, 65, 67, 76, 88, 89, 94

F

fairs, craft 8

fibreboard 20–1, *20*

file 23

fireplace 31, *53*, 76–7, *76, 77*, 92

    hole for 31, 92

flex 50

floor covering 74–5, *74, 75*, 92, 93

flue *57*, 65, 67, 76, 88, 89, 94

framed scene *14*

framework 28–32, *28, 29*, 36

fretsaw 23

front, double hinged 68, *69*

    horizontal *71*

    single removable 68, *72*

    sliding 68, 72

front, opening 27, 65, 68–73, *68, 69, 70, 71, 72, 73*, 94

    papering inside 46

    supporting 39

G

gable ends *65*, 68, 69, *71*, 86, 94

glazing 46, 58, 62

glazing bars 62

H

hallway 19, 33, 38, 45, 81

    mock 34, 36, *36*, *81*

handrail 33, 80, 81

height of rooms 19

hinges 22

    for internal doors 42–4, *42, 43*

for opening front 72, *73*

    pin 44, *44*, 58, *59*

holes for doors *29*, 31, 92, 93

    for fireplace 31, 92

    for windows *29*, 31, 92, 93

I

internal doors 38, 40–4, *41*, 45, 92

internal walls *see* room dividers

J

jigsaw 23

K

knife, craft 23

L

lamps *51*

landing 19, 36, 45, 80, 81, 94

leaded window *59*, 62

light bulbs 50, *51*, 54

    for fire 52, *53*, 54

lights 56, 92, 94

    assembling 52

    in attic 55

    number of 50, 52

    wall 54

loft *see* attic